PUPPET SKITS

Cool Puppet Skits for the Park Patrol to Perform

Noah's Park® Children's Church Puppet Skits (Blue Edition)

© 2002 Cook Communications Ministries. All rights reserved.

Product Developer: Karen Pickering

Managing Editor: Doug Schmidt

Editor: Judy Gillispie

Contributing Writer: Sheila Seifert

Interior Design: Mike Riester

Cover Design: Todd Mock

Illustrations: Aline Heiser
                        Chris Sharp

Photography: © 2001 Cook Communications Ministries
                        by Gaylon Wampler

Published by Cook Communications Ministries
4050 Lee Vance View · Colorado Springs, CO 80918-7100
www.cookministries.com

Printed in Canada.

ISBN: 0-7814-3866-7   101859

TABLE OF CONTENTS

INTRODUCTION

Puppets can be a great addition to a children's ministry program. Through the use of puppets Bible truths can be reinforced and the children can gain a better understanding of how to apply these Bible truths to their own lives.

Two puppets are included in this Children's Church Kit. The puppet personalities are listed on BP·5 of this book. After you identify your puppets and understand their personalities, it can help as you or the Park Patrol members present the puppet skits. (If you would like to purchase additional puppets to use in your program, call 1-800-323-7543 or visit our web site at www.cookministries.com.)

There is one puppet skit provided to correlate with each week's Bible story. For the puppet skit presentation, we suggest that you combine the Elementary and Preschool children. If you have an exceptionally large Children's Church and would like to keep the Elementary and Preschoolers separated for the entire program, you might want to consider having more than one puppet theater and purchasing additional puppets.

You will want to train the Park Patrol members by using the *Park Patrol Training Book*. This training will help them confidently use the puppets and present the skits.

Have fun as you use these puppets and skits. Remember that this is a ministry that can have a great impact on your students!

PERSONALITIES

PONDER the Frog

Ponder the frog is the leader that everyone looks up to in Noah's Park. He watched Noah and Noah's relationship with God and now tries to help the other animals understand how God can help them in their everyday lives. Favorite quote: "I remember the ark!"

HONK the Camel

Honk the purple camel hates dirt; he loves to be clean. Honk is proud of his looks, from his clean and shiny fur to the proud gleam in his eye. Favorite quote: "I'm one good-looking camel."

DREAMER the Rhinoceros

Dreamer the blue rhinoceros is a very sweet and very sleepy animal. Dreamer loves to sleep, loves to dream, and loves to dream about sleeping. Favorite quote: "When I dream, I can do anything!"

STRETCH the Giraffe

Stretch the giraffe is the big sister to all the animals in Noah's Park. She is kind, generous, and very naive. Favorite quote: "I am curious about everything!"

STRETCH

PONDER

DREAMER

HONK

PUPPET THEATERS

Set up your puppet theater in a place apart from the Bible story area or the snacks, games, and crafts areas. That way the Park Patrol members can be setting up and be prepared to perform the day's puppet skit just as soon as you move the children to the puppet skit location. It will also make it obvious to the children that this is a special part of the program.

The following suggestions are given for some simple puppet theaters. Decide on the type of puppet theater by considering the space you have available and the cost of preparation. Be sure to have the puppet theater constructed before working with the Park Patrol for training. They will need to actually use the puppet theater, puppets, and skits as they practice to become proficient for this part of your program.

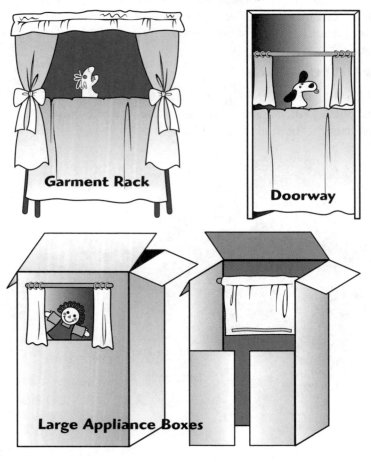

Garment Rack

Doorway

Large Appliance Boxes

BP1: Wrestling to Do Right

Cast: Ponder the Frog, Noah's Park Puppet 2

Props: A small plate with a brownie (or cookie) on it

NP Puppet 2 stares at the brownie, set on the far side of the stage. He moans and groans as Ponder enters. (Note: If you don't have a brownie available, have NP Puppet 2 pretend the brownie is located offstage.)

PONDER: *What's the matter, (Name of Puppet 2)? (Puppet 2 puts hands over eyes and moans again.) What is it, (Name of Puppet 2)? Are you in pain? Where does it hurt? (Ponder searches for an injury.)*

PUPPET 2: *Quick! Hold my hands.*

PONDER: *(Grabs Puppet 2's hands.) Does this help?*

PUPPET 2: *No, but at least I can't grab that brownie. (Points toward brownie.)*

PONDER: *Whose is it?*

PUPPET 2: *Mine. A friend gave me two of them. I ate one and want to save the second for my brother. But he won't be here for a few more minutes.*

PONDER: *How nice of you. God likes it when you care for others in your family.*

PUPPET 2: *I know, but that brownie smells*

awfully good. *(Puppet 2 pulls toward the brownie. Ponder moves with him.)*

PONDER: **Think how much your brother will like it.** *(Ponder pulls Puppet 2 back toward the other side of the stage.)*

PUPPET 2: **He'll like it, but so would I. It would taste so good right now.** *(Puppet 2 pulls toward the brownie. Ponder moves with him.)*

PONDER: **Get a grip on yourself! You can do this!** *(Ponder pulls Puppet 2 back toward the other side of the stage.)*

PUPPET 2: **I can do this. I can do this. I have to remember that I'm doing this for my brother.**

PONDER: **You can show your brother you care by giving it to him. After all, God has given him to you as part of your family.**

PUPPET 2: **And I want to give it to him. So hold me tight, Ponder.**

PONDER: *(Wrestles Puppet 2 toward the opposite side of the stage from the brownie.)* **You're a great brother,** *(Name of Puppet 2).*

PUPPET 2: *(Wrestling.)* **And you're a good friend, Ponder.** *(They wrestle offstage.)* **I thank you! My brother thanks you!** *(Puppet 2's voice fades.)*

BP2: A Hurried Helper

Cast: Ponder the Frog, Noah's Park Puppet 2

Props: Sheet of paper

PONDER: *(Center stage, speaking to the kids)* **Raise your hand if you belong to a family.** *(Waits for kids to answer. Puppet 2 runs behind him from one end of the stage to the other.)* **God gave each of us a family.** *(Puppet 2 runs back across again.)* **People in the Bible had families, too.** *(Puppet 2 runs onstage again and stops by Ponder.)* **Hello,** *(Name of Puppet 2).*

PUPPET 2: **Hi, Ponder.** *(Puppet 2 catches its breath and runs off.)* **See you later.**

PONDER: *(Ponder shrugs and turns back to the kids.)* **Let's see. Where were we?**

PUPPET 2: *(Runs across stage again, this time holding a paper.)* **I'm getting tired.** *(Keeps running.)*

PONDER: *(Calls.)* *(Name of Puppet 2),* **rest for a minute!**

PUPPET 2: *(Comes back.)* **That's a great idea.** *(Panting.)*

PONDER: **What are you doing racing around?**

PUPPET 2: *(Talks quickly.)* **My sister wants to play soccer, so I had to go over to my**

Lesson B2: Families Help One Another | BP•9

aunt's house to ask my mom if my sister could play. My mom told me to go ask my dad. So I went all the way over to Polka-Dot Pond to ask him. Dad wanted to look over the form she has to fill out, so I had to go back to my sister and get the paperwork to show my dad. That's what this is.

PONDER: What a good helper you are. When you help others in your family, it makes God very happy.

PUPPET 2: Maybe that's why God gave me such strong legs.

PONDER: What do you mean?

PUPPET 2: He knew I'd have to do a lot of running to be a helper in my family. I'd better go now. Bye, Ponder. (Ponder waves. Puppet 2 runs off stage. In a second he runs back the other way yelling.) **Dad said yes, Sis! He said you could join the team!** (Runs off stage.)

BP3: Remember the Rules

Cast: Ponder the Frog, Noah's Park Puppet 2

PUPPET 2: *Ponder, I'm so scared.*

PONDER: *About what?*

PUPPET 2: *I'm going to meet my new Sunday school teacher tomorrow. My old teacher had a baby so she won't be there for a long time. So, now I have a brand-new Sunday school teacher.*

PONDER: *And she scares you?*

PUPPET 2: *No. I don't know. I've never met her. But what if I do something wrong? How can I remember to do everything right?*

PONDER: *What are you trying to remember?*

PUPPET 2: *Everything my parents have taught me.*

PONDER: *Like what?*

PUPPET 2: *(Talks quickly.)* **Don't talk with your mouth full. Don't run near the Polka Dot Pond. Speak clearly. Take turns. Don't interrupt. Clean my room. Pick up after myself. Don't climb Nosy Rock. Share. Don't laugh with your mouth full. Don't burp. Don't pick your nose. Eat one bite**

	at a time. Eat all your food. Share your toys—
PONDER:	*(Interrupting.)* **No wonder you're scared. You've learned a lot from your parents.**
PUPPET 2:	**What am I going to do, Ponder? I can't remember everything!**
PONDER:	**You don't have to remember everything,** *(Name of Puppet 2).* **Just remember that your family loves you, and God gave you a family so that if you have any questions, you can ask them.**
PUPPET 2:	**You're right. They'd help me, wouldn't they? I'll have to remember that I can ask them.**
PONDER:	**Stop worrying . . . and quit slouching. Stand up straight. Comb your hair.** *(Puppet 2 looks at Ponder.)* **Just kidding!** *(Both puppets laugh.)* **I think your new teacher will like you just fine.** *(Both puppets leave the stage together.)*

BP4: See What Love Is

Cast: Ponder the Frog, Noah's Park Puppet 2

Ponder is onstage and Puppet 2 comes out with its hands over its eyes. Puppet 2 runs into Ponder.

PONDER: *Ouch!*

PUPPET 2: *(With eyes still covered.)* **Oh! Sorry, I didn't see you.**

PONDER: **Then maybe you should take your hands off your eyes.**

PUPPET 2: *(Uncovers eyes.)* **But I'm going home to see my family.**

PONDER: *(Looks at the kids and then back at Puppet 2.)* **I don't understand.**

PUPPET 2: **I love my family.**

PONDER: **Yeah.**

PUPPET 2: **I want to show them how much I love them.**

PONDER: **Yeah.**

PUPPET 2: **And love is blind.**

PONDER: *(Scratches head.)* **Yeah?**

PUPPET 2: **So I'm covering my eyes with my hands.** *(Puppet 2 covers its eyes with its hands and bumps into Ponder again.)*

PONDER: **But you won't be able to see where you're going.**

PUPPET 2: *It's just a form of tough love, I guess.* (Peeks out.)

PONDER: (Name of Puppet 2), **when people say that love is blind, it means that when someone in your family does something mean to you, you forgive them.**

PUPPET 2: (Uncovers eyes all the way.) **Really?**

PONDER: **Really.**

PUPPET 2: **You mean I don't have to cover my eyes?**

PONDER: **No, all you have to do is forgive when someone is mean to you and think about how you can not be mean back.**

PUPPET 2: **Great! I wasn't sure how I was going to walk all the way home without being able to see.**

PONDER: **I'm proud of you,** (Name of Puppet 2), **for doing your best to love the family God gave you. Not only can you use your eyes, but I'll also walk with you to make sure you get home in one piece.** (They both walk off together.)

BP5: All My Best Friends

Cast: Ponder the Frog, Noah's Park Puppet 2

Note: In the opening line, when Puppet 2 speaks, leave out the name of whichever puppet you are using so he is not talking about himself.

Ponder and Puppet 2 are onstage.

PUPPET 2: *What am I going to do? Honk, Dreamer, Stretch, and Ivory are my friends. And Screech, Shadow, Howler, Flutter, and you are my friends, too. What am I going to do?*

PONDER: *I don't see your problem.*

PUPPET 2: *I have so many friends!*

PONDER: *Isn't it a good thing that God gave you friends?*

PUPPET 2: *Of course it is, but I have so many.*

PONDER: *I don't think you can have too many friends.*

PUPPET 2: *But I have so many friends that I don't know which friend is my BEST friend. What am I going to do?*

PONDER: *(Name of Puppet 2),* **aren't all of your friends special?**

PUPPET 2: *Yes, they are. Each one is so special that I don't know how I'll ever pick a best friend! What am I going to do?*

PONDER: *You don't have to do anything. You don't need to choose one best friend. You can love each of your friends the best way you can.*

PUPPET 2: *Are you sure I don't have to choose one best friend?*

PONDER: *Positive. You can love all of your friends extra specially. It's also more fun that way.*

PUPPET 2: *What a relief! But what if one of my friends asks if I'll be their best friend?*

PONDER: *Then you tell them that you would love for them to be one of your eight best friends.*

PUPPET 2: *I never thought of that. Instead of only one best friend, I can have eight or ten or one hundred best friends. I'm so happy, because I really love all of my friends.*

PONDER: *And we love you,* (Name of Puppet 2). *Let's go find the others.*

PUPPET 2: *That's a great idea. Let's go and ask them—all of them—to be our very best friends.* (They exit.)

BP6: Jesus Is My Special Friend

Cast: Ponder the Frog, Noah's Park Puppet 2

Props: Jump rope or string

Tie one end of the rope or string offstage. Puppet 2 is onstage, holding the other end.

PUPPET 2: *Okay, Jesus, it's Your turn to hold the jump rope. (Pauses.) Jesus?*

PONDER: *(Enters.)* **Who are you talking to?**

PUPPET 2: *Jesus. He's my special friend. I want to play jump rope with Him. So I tied one end of the rope to that tree over there and have twirled it for five minutes. Now it's Jesus' turn to twirl it for me.*

PONDER: *Jesus isn't going to twirl your jump rope.*

PUPPET 2: *If He's my special friend He should. (Calling.) Jesus! It's Your turn to twirl the jump rope.*

PONDER: *(Name of Puppet 2),* **Jesus isn't going to twirl the rope for you. But He's still your friend, and He loves you very much.**

PUPPET 2: *But I want to play jump rope with a special friend.*

PONDER: *Isn't your cousin one of your special friends?*

PUPPET 2: Yes.

PONDER: Why isn't he twirling the end of your jump rope?

PUPPET 2: Don't be silly.

PONDER: I'm not being any more silly than you are. Jesus IS a special friend, but in a different way than your other friends. Maybe He sent me to hold the end of the rope for you.

PUPPET 2: He told you to play with me?

PONDER: He told me to love those around me. Since you want to play jump rope, and friends help each other, I'm going to twirl the rope for you.

PUPPET 2: (Ponder twirls the rope. Puppet 2 jumps up and down behind it to give the illusion of rope-jumping and chants in rhythm.)
Jesus is my
Special friend.
Jesus loves me.
Say it again!

PONDER: Kids, let's say the jump rope rhyme with (Name of Puppet 2). "Jesus is my special friend. Jesus helps me. Say it again." (Repeat the rhyme a few times.)

PUPPET 2: Thanks, kids. Thanks, Ponder. That was fun.

(Exit.)

BP7: Simon Says Help Your Friends

Cast: Ponder the Frog, Noah's Park Puppet 2

Ponder and Puppet 2 come onstage.

PONDER: *Hey, kids, let's play "Simon Says."*

PUPPET 2: *Ponder is Simon. He'll tell us to do things, and we'll do them only if he says "Simon Says" first.*

PONDER: *And if you don't make any mistakes, you win! Ready? Simon says put your hands in the air.* (Ponder and Puppet 2 put their hands in the air.) *Simon says touch your nose.* (Ponder and Puppet 2 touch their noses.) *Now put your hands on your head.* (Ponder puts hands on his head.)

PUPPET 2: *Wait! Don't put your hands on your head, kids! Ponder didn't say, "Simon says," so don't do it.*

PONDER: *(Name of Puppet 2), you're not going to win this game of "Simon Says" if you warn the kids.*

PUPPET 2: *Maybe not, but these kids are my friends. And friends help each other.*

PONDER: *Hmmm. (Shakes head.) Well, let's keep going. Simon says wiggle your hands.* (Ponder and Puppet 2 wiggle their hands.) *Simon says stand up.* (Ponder and Puppet 2 rise up taller as if standing.) *Simon says sit down.* (Ponder and

Puppet 2 lower down as if sitting.) **Stand up.** *(Ponder straightens up.)*

PUPPET 2: **No, no, kids! Stay down! Ponder didn't say, "Simon says."**

PONDER: *(Name of Puppet 2)*, **don't you care about winning?**

PUPPET 2: **Well, yes, but some of my friends are confused, and I want to help them. We really are good friends, even though I'm an animal and they're kids.**

PONDER: **Well, I suppose you're right. Friends are very special. God does give them to us. Maybe there's a way ALL the friends can win this game.**

PUPPET 2: **I think so too. Are you ready to play again, Ponder?**

PONDER: **Simon says stand up.** *(Ponder and Puppet 2 rise.)* **Simon says turn around.** *(Ponder and Puppet 2 turn around.)* **Simon says fold your hands together.** *(Ponder and Puppet 2 put their hands together.)* **Simon says sit down.** *(Ponder and Puppet 2 lower.)* **Simon says smile.** *(Ponder and Puppet 2 nod their heads as if smiling.)* **Now unfold your hands.**

PUPPET 2: **Wait! Remember, Ponder didn't say, "Simon Says."**

PONDER: **Well done,** *(Name of Puppet 2).* **Great game everyone! You all won!**

(Exit.)

BP8: That's Not All

Cast: Ponder the Frog, Noah's Park Puppet 2

Note: If the script for Puppet 2 names the same puppet you are using, change the name to another Noah's Park puppet.

Ponder and Puppet 2 are onstage.

PUPPET 2: *(Hopping from one side of Ponder to the other.)* **You'll never guess what Jesus did for my friends!**

PONDER: **What did He do?**

PUPPET 2: **The other day, Screech fell out of a tree and scraped his knee. Then it scabbed up, and now it's gone. Jesus healed Screech's knee.**

PONDER: **God did make our bodies to heal.**

PUPPET 2: *(Hopping up and down.)* **That's not all!**

PONDER: **How else did Jesus help your friends?**

PUPPET 2: **Flutter was feeling lonely. So, Ivory went over to play with her.**

PONDER: **God gives us friends for many reasons.**

PUPPET 2: *(Hopping.)* **But that's not all.**

PONDER: **How else has Jesus helped your friends?**

PUPPET 2: **Well, Honk was worried every night**

about kids hiding under his bed.

PONDER: *Kids? Do you mean that since some KIDS worry about imaginary ANIMALS under their beds, now here's an ANIMAL that worries about KIDS under the bed? That's funny.*

PUPPET 2: *Yeah, but then his dad started singing "Jesus Loves Me" with him every night at bedtime. Now he falls asleep humming that song, and he's not scared any more.* (Hopping.) *It's great!*

PONDER: *Wow! That's a way Jesus helped. Anything else?*

PUPPET 2: (Stops hopping.) *I guess that's all.*

PONDER: *Well, I have a surprise for you. That's NOT all. Look at all those kids sitting out there. They are all your friends. And Jesus is so strong and loving that He can help every single one of them with any problem too.*

PUPPET 2: *Jesus can help every single one of them? Are you sure?*

PONDER: *I'm sure. Jesus can help them with all of their problems.*

PUPPET 2: (Starts hopping again.) *Wow! That's amazing! Jesus sure is a great friend!* (Exit.)

BP9: Who's the Best at Sharing?

Cast: Ponder the Frog, Noah's Park Puppet 2

Props: A small toy

Puppet 2, with a toy in its hands, runs onstage to where Ponder is standing.

PUPPET 2: *Quick, Ponder, hide this toy for me.*

PONDER: *What's the matter?*

PUPPET 2: *Shadow wants to play with it, and I don't want him to.*

PONDER: *Were you going to play with it?*

PUPPET 2: *Not right now, but I want to play with it in a few years. Quick, hide it, so Shadow won't be able to find it.*

PONDER: *(Name of Puppet 2),* **did you know that one of the reasons God gives us friends is so we'll learn to share our things with them?**

PUPPET 2: *I don't want to share.*

PONDER: *If Shadow had a toy that he wasn't playing with, wouldn't you want him to share it with you?*

PUPPET 2: *Well, yes, but this is MY toy. Why should I let Shadow play with my toy? It's mine. It belongs to me.*

PONDER: *What if God said that? What if He said, "The sun is mine. It belongs to me. I made it. I'm not going to share it with anyone!"*

PUPPET 2: *We wouldn't have light or heat or things to eat.*

PONDER: *Or what if God said, "Those plants are mine. And that water's mine. I'm not sharing them with anyone!"*

PUPPET 2: *That wouldn't be very good at all.*

PONDER: *That's true. Think about it,* (Name of Puppet 2). *If God's willing to share His things with us, shouldn't you share yours with others?*

PUPPET 2: *I think you're right. I think I'd LIKE to follow God's example of friendship.*

PONDER: *Are you're going to share?*

PUPPET 2: *Yes. Shadow is my friend, and I'd like him to know that.* (Yells offstage.) *Shadow! You can play with my toy now. But you have to give it back when you're done so I can play with it in a few years.* (Runs offstage.)

BP10: Drumming Up a Story

Cast: Ponder the Frog, Noah's Park Puppet 2, Leader or Park Patrol actor

Props: A Bible

Puppet 2 has Bible in front of him onstage.

PUPPET 2: *(Pretends to play drums on the Bible.)* **Rat-a-tat-tat. Rat-a-tat-tat.**

PONDER: *(Enters, not having seen what Puppet 2 was doing.)* **What are you doing,** *(Name of Puppet 2)***?**

PUPPET 2: **Having fun!** *(Points to the Bible.)*

LEADER: *(Enters, not having seen what Puppet 2 was doing.)* **There's my Bible!**

PUPPET 2: **Hello,** *(Name of Leader)***. You left your Bible in church last Sunday. I told my parents that I'd bring it to you.**

LEADER: **Thanks,** *(Name of Puppet 2)***. I've missed it.**

PUPPET 2: **I would miss it too. My parents told me that I could learn so much from the Bible. They were right!**

PONDER: **That's so wise,** *(Name of Puppet 2)***. What did you learn from** *(Name of Leader)***'s Bible this week?**

PUPPET 2: **So many things that I wouldn't know where to start. Like I learned that if you drop this Bible from the tallest tree in Screech's Hollow, it**

takes two seconds before it hits the ground. *(Leader and Ponder look aghast.)* **And if you hit it hard, it makes a loud drum sound. And if you . . .**

PONDER: **Hold on,** *(Name of Puppet 2).* **That isn't what your parents meant about learning from the Bible.**

LEADER: *(Picks up Bible and caringly dusts it off.)* *(Name of Puppet 2),* **that isn't how you treat a Bible—because it's a very special book. God gave it to us.**

PUPPET 2: **Oh, sorry. You mean I shouldn't play the drums on it?**

LEADER: **That's a good start.**

PUPPET 2: **Um, then what do you think my parents meant?**

LEADER: *(Opens Bible.)* **To learn from the Bible, you have to OPEN it and read it or have someone read it to you. That's how God's people learn about God and the right way to live—from the stories inside of it.**

PUPPET 2: **This book is filled with stories?**

PONDER: *(Name of Puppet 2),* **let's find a tall shade tree in Screech's Hollow. But this time we'll sit UNDER it, and I'll read you some Bible stories.**

PUPPET 2: **I love stories. Are they good ones? I can't wait to hear them. Let's go!**

(All three exit together.)

BP11: A Free Offering

Cast: Ponder the Frog, Noah's Park Puppet 2

Props: Two tall stacks of coins, a piece of paper

Puppet 2 is looking at the two stacks of coins that are in front of it.

PUPPET 2: *(Talking to self.)* **I finally have enough money to buy a huge bag of candy.**

PONDER: *(Enters with a paper held up to its face.)* **Unbelievable!**

PUPPET 2: **Hi, Ponder. What's unbelievable?**

PONDER: **Hi,** *(Name of Puppet 2).* **There's a little girl who will die if she doesn't get an operation.**

PUPPET 2: **That's so sad.**

PONDER: **It says that she became a Christian because missionaries told her about Jesus.**

PUPPET 2: **That's great!**

PONDER: **If only her family had enough money for the operation.**

PUPPET 2: **That's so sad.**

PONDER: **The church that sent the missionaries is going to raise money.**

PUPPET 2: **That's great! Who are they going to get the money from?**

PONDER: **From anyone who wants to give it, anyone who cares what happens to**

this little girl.

PUPPET 2: *I care.*

PONDER: **You can give an extra offering to that church if you want.**

PUPPET 2: **You mean give my money?**

PONDER: **If you want.**

PUPPET 2: **You mean money that belongs to ME?**

PONDER: *It's your choice.*

PUPPET 2: **But this money belongs to me.**

PONDER: **You don't have to give it unless you want to. When God's people give offerings to the church, the church uses it to help others.**

PUPPET 2: *(Looks back and forth between the stacks of money.)* **I was going to buy candy.**

PONDER: **No one is forcing you. An offering is something you give freely.**

PUPPET 2: *(Sighs.)* **I really want to eat candy, but if I needed an operation, I'd want people to give money to help me. So . . . I'll share my money.** *(Pushes one stack of coins toward Ponder.)* **Who should I give this to?**

PONDER: **I'm proud of you,** *(Name of Puppet 2).* **Let's find something to put your money in, and then I'll show you who to give it to.** *(Exit.)*

BP12: Cool Prayers

Cast: Ponder the Frog, Noah's Park Puppet 2, Leader or Park Patrol actor

Note: If you know that someone from your children's church group is absent due to illness today, you may name that person in the script and pray for him or her at the end.

Ponder and Puppet 2 are onstage.

PONDER: *You're exaggerating!*

PUPPET 2: *I'm not. It's bad, real bad.*

PONDER: *Are you sure?*

PUPPET 2: *That's what my mother told me. One of our friends isn't here at church today because she is really sick.*

LEADER: *(Enters.)* **What's the matter? You both look so down.**

PONDER: *One of our friends is sick.*

PUPPET 2: *So sick.*

PONDER: *We feel so bad.*

PUPPET 2: *I wish I could do something to help.*

LEADER: *The best thing that we can do is to pray for that person.*

PONDER: *True. Praying is something special we can do.*

PUPPET 2: *So when someone is sick, and only when they're sick, we should pray for them?*

PONDER: *People can pray for other people about any needs they have.*

LEADER: *We can also thank God for things anytime we want to.*

PUPPET 2: *I know that our sick friend from church needs prayer, but do you think there are other people in this room who would like prayer also?*

PONDER: *There probably are. The kids might have prayer requests too.*

PUPPET 2: *That would be so cool to see God's people—that's you, kids—praying for each other.*

PONDER: *It's a very good thing to pray and thank God when you're together.*

LEADER: *Does anyone want me to pray for them, or to pray for someone you know, or to tell God thanks for something?* (Listen to the kids' prayer requests. Then the Leader should lead a prayer for all the prayer requests given.)

PUPPET 2: *That is so cool when God's people pray for each other. It gives me goose bumps!*

BP13: Forgotten and Forgiven

Cast: Ponder the Frog, Noah's Park Puppet 2

Note: If the Leader's name you choose for this skit is a male, change the appropriate pronouns in the script.

Ponder is onstage. Puppet 2 runs onstage.

PUPPET 2: *(Runs about.)* **What am I going to do?**

PONDER: **What's the matter,** *(Name of Puppet 2)***?**

PUPPET 2: **I don't know how to tell you this.**

PONDER: **Tell me what?**

PUPPET 2: **I don't know my lines. I had the script, and I meant to memorize my lines, but I went to play with Flutter, and I forgot my script, and now I have no idea what I'm supposed to say.** *(Leader's name)* **is going to be so upset with me. What am I going to do?**

PONDER: **You need to tell** *(Leader's name)* **what happened.**

PUPPET 2: **I can't. She might yell at me.**

PONDER: **She's not going to yell at you.**

PUPPET 2: **She might say I can't ever be in a puppet skit in Children's Church again.**

PONDER: **She won't say that. Leaders are not in the church to be mean to us.** *(Leader's name)* **cares for you.**

PUPPET 2: **But I let her down.**

PONDER: *Yes, you did.*

PUPPET 2: *I won't be able to say any of the words that she wrote for me to say.*

PONDER: *You're right, you won't. But she'll forgive you. Because you made a mistake, it doesn't mean that* (Leader's name) *will stop liking you or trying to help you.*

PUPPET 2: *It doesn't?*

PONDER: *Of course not.* (Leader's name) *and the pastor of this church and other church leaders ENJOY people. And they know that everyone makes a mistake once in a while. They may be disappointed, but they work very hard to care for each person here.*

PUPPET 2: *So, what should I do?*

PONDER: (Leader's name) *is over there. You need to go and tell her what you told me. Then tell her that you're sorry.*

PUPPET 2: *I AM sorry. I am really, really, really sorry.*

PONDER: *Go and tell her.*

PUPPET 2: *Okay.*

PONDER: *Would you like me to go with you?*

PUPPET 2: *Yes, I would. Thanks, Ponder. You're a real friend.* (Exit.)

BP14: The Messenger

Cast: Ponder the Frog, Noah's Park Puppet 2

Ponder and Puppet 2 are onstage.

PONDER: *(Name of Puppet 2)*, **what are you going to do this weekend?**

PUPPET 2: **Nothing much, but my aunt is coming to visit.**

PONDER: **Is that a good thing?**

PUPPET 2: **Yes. She's going to tell me when my cousin can come over and play.**

PONDER: **Your cousin isn't coming with your aunt?**

PUPPET 2: **No, he's sick. He's staying home with my uncle. Only my aunt is coming this time.**

PONDER: **How far away do they live?**

PUPPET 2: **It takes them four hours to walk here.**

PONDER: **Whew! That is quite a walk! Wait. If your aunt isn't here yet, how did you find out that your cousin is sick and can't come with her?**

PUPPET 2: **Well, a friend of theirs told a friend of mine that my cousin wouldn't be coming. But I don't know the whole story or when my cousin will finally be able to come. But my aunt**

knows everything and is going to bring me the message.

PONDER: *So, your aunt is the messenger.*

PUPPET 2: *Yes.*

PONDER: *She's the messenger of a message that is going to make you really happy.*

PUPPET 2: *Yes. My aunt will have the story right. She'll know when my cousin's coming.*

PONDER: *(Laughs.)* **Your aunt is like the angel who told Mary and Joseph that Jesus was coming. People had known for a long, long time that God was going to send a Savior. But no one knew just when. Or how! The angels came with God's message. They were the messengers who told Mary and Joseph what was really going to happen.**

PUPPET 2: *I'll bet they were as anxious to hear the angel's message as I am to hear my aunt's message.*

PONDER: *Perhaps even more. Look over there. Who's that way over there?*

PUPPET 2: *That's my aunt. She's here! I've got to go now, Ponder. Bye!* (Heads offstage, calling.) **Oh Auntie! Auntie! When is my cousin coming to visit? Oh, Auntie!** (Exits.)

BP15: A Birthday Party

Cast: Ponder the Frog, Noah's Park Puppet 2

Props: Birthday party hat for Ponder, a few streamers to decorate stage, stack of envelopes off to the side

Ponder, wearing a party hat, is pretending to hang up a streamer.

PUPPET 2: *(Enters and looks around.)* **This looks great! Are you getting ready for a party?**

PONDER: *Yes, I am.*

PUPPET 2: **You have streamers, party hats, and balloons in back. I love balloons. That red one is my favorite. What kind of party are you getting ready for?**

PONDER: *A birthday party.*

PUPPET 2: **Do you have cake and ice cream, too?**

PONDER: *I sure do.*

PUPPET 2: **Whose birthday is it?**

PONDER: *It's the birthday of God's Son!*

PUPPET 2: **Well, I think you're mixed up. It's Christmas, Ponder! But this isn't a CHRISTMAS party. You're having a BIRTHDAY party.**

PONDER: *That's right. On my birthday,*

everyone celebrates that I was born.

PUPPET 2:   *Me, too. Only they do it on my birthday.*

PONDER: *This year, I decided to celebrate that Jesus was born by throwing Him a BIRTHDAY party.*

PUPPET 2:   *What a great idea! Can I come?*

PONDER: *Most definitely. All the animals in the park are invited.*

PUPPET 2:   *This is going to be the best Christmas—I mean birthday party ever! I'll tell everyone I see that it's Jesus' birthday.*

PONDER: *Great idea,* (Name of Puppet 2). *Everyone should know that God's Son was born. I have a stack of invitations over there. Would you like to pass them out to all the animals for me?*

PUPPET 2:   *I'd love to.* (Looks offstage and calls.) *Hey, Flutter! Stay right there!* (Gets an invitation and begins to move offstage, still calling.) *You're invited to a birthday party for Jesus! I hope you can come . . .* (Exits.)

BP16: He's Here!

Cast: Ponder the Frog, Noah's Park Puppet 2

Props: Puppet-size sunglasses, a tiny umbrella or piece of colorful cloth to serve as a puppet-size beach towel

Ponder is wearing sunglasses, lying on a beach towel or under a beach umbrella.

PONDER: *(Sits up.)* **Hi, kids. It's so nice to see you. I love quiet days at the pond like today. They're so relaxing.** *(Yawns and lies down.)*

PUPPET 2: *(Running onstage.)* **Ponder! Ponder! Where are you?** *(Runs to Ponder and shakes him.)*

PONDER: *(To kids.)* **So much for my quiet day!** *(Sits up. To Puppet 2.)* **What's all the excitement about,** *(Name of Puppet 2)***?**

PUPPET 2: **You'll never guess what just happened! He's here!**

PONDER: **Who's here?**

PUPPET 2: **My brother's here. He's really here!**

PONDER: **I didn't know you had a brother.**

PUPPET 2: **I didn't, but now I do. My mother had a baby. The baby's my new brother. He's here! He's here! I'm so excited. I had to tell you first. Now I'll have someone to play with, laugh with, and tell stories to. We're going to be such good friends.**

PONDER: *I'm sure you will be. That good news is worth interrupting a quiet day. Your excitement reminds me of how the angels must have felt.*

PUPPET 2: *What angels?*

PONDER: *The angels who were so full of the good news that Jesus, God's Son, was born. They shared their good news with shepherds, who were on the hillside watching their sheep.*

PUPPET 2: *What did the angels say? Did they say what I said? Did they say, "He's here!"?*

PONDER: *They said something very close to that. They invited the shepherds to go and see baby Jesus for themselves. They were full of joy— and so were the shepherds!*

PUPPET 2: *Did the shepherds go to see baby Jesus?*

PONDER: *Yes, they did. And I am going to come see your new baby too.*

PUPPET 2: *You are?*

PONDER: *I am. You're so excited, that you've made me excited too. I can't just sit here now.*

PUPPET 2: *Come on then! You're going to love him. He's so cute. I love him already. I really do . . .* (Both exit with Puppet 2 excitedly babbling.)

BP17: Just Like Dad

Cast: Ponder the Frog, Noah's Park Puppet 2

PONDER: *You look just like your dad.*

PUPPET 2: *You think so?*

PONDER: *I know so. Your eyes are the same color and shape that his are.*

PUPPET 2: *You're right. My eyes are like his.*

PONDER: *And your smile curves in the same way that his does.*

PUPPET 2: *We do smile a lot. You're not the only one who thinks my dad and I look alike. Other animals have told me that too.*

PONDER: *It's not just on the outside either. You two have the same habits and sense of humor.*

PUPPET 2: *We are a lot alike.*

PONDER: *A whole lot.*

PUPPET 2: *Do you think Jesus was like His Father?*

PONDER: *Definitely.*

PUPPET 2: *So if Joseph had dark hair, do you think Jesus had dark hair too?*

PONDER: *Joseph loved Jesus very much, but he wasn't Jesus' father.*

PUPPET 2: *He wasn't? Then who was?*

PONDER: *Jesus is GOD's Son.*

PUPPET 2: *God is Jesus' Dad?*

PONDER: *Yes, and Jesus looked a lot like His Father.*

PUPPET 2: *So if Jesus had dark hair, then that means that God has dark hair too?*

PONDER: *(Laughs.)* *That's not what I mean! What I mean is that Jesus is God, too.*

PUPPET 2: *Oh, I get it. Because Jesus is God's Son, we can know what God is like by learning about Jesus!*

PONDER: *Exactly!*

BP18: Look Out!

Cast: Ponder the Frog, Noah's Park Puppet 2

Ponder and Puppet 2 are onstage. (Use a puppet other than Ivory for Puppet 2.)

PONDER: *Quick, (Name of Puppet 2),* **move over here!** *(Ponder pulls Puppet 2 across the stage.)*

PUPPET 2: *(Looks around.)* **Where did that water come from? Is it raining? If you hadn't told me to move, I'd have gotten wet.**

PONDER: **Personally, I don't mind getting wet.**

PUPPET 2: **That's because you're a frog.**

PONDER: **But I do mind being sprayed by Ivory the Elephant.** *(Looks up.)* **Look out! Move here!** *(They rush to the middle of the stage.)*

PUPPET 2: **That water almost hit us again. Why is Ivory spraying us?**

PONDER: **Ivory isn't spraying us on purpose. Ivory's trying to get those bananas from the tree.** *(Points up.)* **But the bananas are too high. Quick, over here!** *(They rush to the other side of the stage.)*

PUPPET 2: **That was a close one. Let me see if I have this right. You're getting**

sprayed with water because bananas are too high in a tree?

PONDER: *That's right.*

PUPPET 2: *That doesn't make any sense at all.*

PONDER: *Ivory is spraying water at the bananas in the tree to try and make them fall down, so she can eat them. But once the water hits the bananas, the water sprays down on anyone in the area. (Looks up.) Move again! (They rush across the stage.)*

PUPPET 2: *Ponder, thanks for looking out for me so I don't get wet. You're taking care of me just as God took care of Jesus.*

PONDER: *Look out! (They both hop one step toward the middle.)*

PUPPET 2: *God placed people around Jesus to help keep Him safe.*

PONDER: *That's true. God helped Jesus grow and learn through others. And He places people around US to keep us safe. (Looks up.) Oh no! Look out! A bunch of bananas is headed our way. Run for it! (Both puppets run across the stage and exit.)*

BP19: Learning to Hop

Cast: Ponder the Frog, Noah's Park Puppet 2

Puppet 2 is bouncing around the stage.

PUPPET 2: **I can hop on one foot.** *(Bounces while leaning to one side as if on one foot and then falls down.)* **I CAN do this.** *(Gets up, bounces, and falls down.)* **I can hop on one foot. I can. I can.** *(Bounces and falls down.)* **It's no use. Hey, kids. Do you know how to hop on one foot?** *(Waits for answer.)* **Would you show me how to hop on one foot?** *(Watches kids hop.)* **That's really good. Okay, sit back down. Listen: I know my alphabet, I know "Jesus Loves the Little Children" by heart, and I know how to clean my bedroom. I just can't hop on one foot. YOU were great at hopping. I wish I were like you.**

PONDER: *(Enters.)* *(Name of Puppet 2),* **you have a great voice. I didn't know you could sing until I heard you yesterday.**

PUPPET 2: **Singing isn't a big deal. I want to learn to hop on one foot like these kids, but I can't.**

PONDER: **Let me see.**

PUPPET 2: (Bounces and falls down.) **Can you hop, Ponder?**

PONDER: **Of course.** (Ponder hops around the stage.) **I'm a frog.**

PUPPET 2: **I wish I were you.**

PONDER: **No, you don't. If you were me, you'd croak instead of singing like you do.**

PUPPET 2: **Singing is easy.**

PONDER: **For you, but not for me.**

PUPPET 2: **I'll bet Jesus never had these kinds of problems when He was a kid.**

PONDER: **I'll bet He did. He had to grow up and learn things just like us.**

PUPPET 2: **Do you think He ever learned to hop on one foot?**

PONDER: **If He did, He learned the same way you're learning—by practice. Try it again.**

PUPPET 2: **Okay, here goes.** (Puppet 2 hops offstage. There is a loud crash.) **Ow!**

PONDER: **That looks like it hurt. I'm coming,** (Name of Puppet 2)**!**

(Exit.)

BP20: The Best Birthday Gift

Cast: Ponder the Frog, Noah's Park Puppet 2

Puppet 2 is onstage talking to the kids.

PUPPET 2: *(Points to one of the kids.)* **What is one thing that someone in your family does that makes you happy?** *(Listens.)* **That would make me happy too.** *(Points to another kid.)* **What is one thing that makes you happy?** *(Listens.)* **That would make me happy too.** *(Ponder enters.)* **Ponder, what is one thing that makes you happy?**

PONDER: **Seeing you talk to all these great kids.**

PUPPET 2: **Really? How does that please you?**

PONDER: **I enjoy seeing my friends with friends.**

PUPPET 2: **Hmmm. That doesn't help me.**

PONDER: **Help you what?**

PUPPET 2: **My dad's birthday is coming up, and I want to give him something or do something that will really make him happy.**

PONDER: **Did you ask your mother what your dad would like?**

PUPPET 2: **Yes. She told me to just be ME and do whatever Dad wants to do on his birthday.**

PONDER: *And you don't want to do that?*

PUPPET 2: *It's not that I don't want to. What she said doesn't sound very exciting. I want to give him the BEST birthday gift. I want to do something really special for my dad. What do you think Jesus would do?*

PONDER: *Well, Jesus did please God, His Father.*

PUPPET 2: *How did He do that? I'm sure that whatever He did to please God will also make my dad happy.*

PONDER: *Jesus did what God told him to do.*

PUPPET 2: *Is that all?*

PONDER: *That's it. Jesus listened to God.*

PUPPET 2: *Maybe my mother was right. If Jesus listened to His Dad—God—then I'll listen to God too—AND my dad.*

PONDER: *That would be a great gift,* (name of Puppet 2).

PUPPET 2: *I guess I only have one problem left.*

PONDER: *What's that?*

PUPPET 2: *How do I wrap it up?*

(Exit.)

BP21: Follow the Leader

Cast: Ponder the Frog, Noah's Park Puppet 2

Ponder and Puppet 2 are next to each other onstage.

PONDER: *Okay, (Name of Puppet 2), **it's your turn to be the leader.***

PUPPET 2: ***Scoop to the right.*** *(Puppet 2 flings out an arm, bends to the right, and makes a scooping motion.)*

PONDER: ***I'll scoop to the right.*** *(Imitates Puppet 2.)*

PUPPET 2: ***Scoop to the left!*** *(Turns and does the same action with the left arm.)*

PONDER: ***Scoop to the left.*** *(Imitates Puppet 2.)*

PUPPET 2: *(Turning in a circle while jumping.)* ***Jump. Jump. Jump. Jump.*** *(Ponder turns and jumps next to Puppet 2.)* ***Bow down low. Reach up high.*** *(Ponder imitates Puppet 2.)* ***You're a great follower, Ponder.***

PONDER: *I've had practice.*

PUPPET 2: *Who have you been playing with?*

PONDER: *Jesus.*

PUPPET 2: *Jesus doesn't play "Follow the Leader."*

PONDER: *Not like we were, but He does tell us, "Follow me."*

PUPPET 2: *He wants us to follow Him like you're following me?*

PONDER: *Exactly. And once we learn to follow Jesus, then we can be better helpers to those around us.*

PUPPET 2: *That is so cool! Whenever I hear anything about Jesus, I'm going to listen real closely so that I'll be the best at following Him as the Leader.*

PONDER: *That's good,* (Puppet 2)*. I think Jesus is going to like playing "Follow the Leader" with you.*

PUPPET 2: *Okay, now it's your turn.*

PONDER: *Again? Okay.* (Yawns.) *I'm going to lean right here against this side of the stage, and you can lean against that side of the stage.* (Leans against the stage or lies down if stage has no side post.)

PUPPET 2: (Leans on opposite side.) *Now what?*

PONDER: *We both cover our eyes.*

PUPPET 2: *I'm covering my eyes with my hands. What's next?*

PONDER: (Yawns.) *Now we take a little nap. I'm tired. Good night,* (Name of Puppet 2)*.*

BP22: A Gazillion Needs

Cast: Ponder the Frog, Noah's Park Puppet 2

Ponder and Puppet 2 are onstage.

PUPPET 2: *Tell me something to do. I can do just about anything.*

PONDER: *I don't know.*

PUPPET 2: *Try me. Tell me what to do.*

PONDER: *Okay, take one hand and rub your stomach.*

PUPPET 2: *(Puppet 2 rubs its stomach.)* **Done!**

PONDER: *Now with your other hand, pat your head.*

PUPPET 2: *(Puppet 2 pats its head while still rubbing stomach.)* **Done! Sort of.**

PONDER: *Now jump up and down.*

PUPPET 2: *(Puppet 2 jumps up and down while rubbing stomach and patting head.)* **Done! I'm good at this, aren't I?**

PONDER: *Now bend to the right and then to the left.*

PUPPET 2: *(Puppet 2 tries to rub stomach, pat head, jump, and bend all at the same time, cannot do them all.)* **This is hard.**

PONDER: *It looks hard.*

PUPPET 2: *(Still trying.)* **Maybe I can only do a few things at once.**

PONDER: *Aren't you glad that Jesus doesn't say things like that?*

PUPPET 2: *How many things can Jesus do at one time?* (Keeps trying.)

PONDER: *Jesus can take care of everyone's needs all at the same time.*

PUPPET 2: (Stops.) *You're kidding me.*

PONDER: *No.*

PUPPET 2: *But that's like a gazillion different things at once.*

PONDER: *Or more.*

PUPPET 2: *How can He do that?*

PONDER: *He's God.*

PUPPET 2: *Why would He want to do that?*

PONDER: *He cares about our needs and likes taking care of us.*

PUPPET 2: *That's it!*

PONDER: *What's it?*

PUPPET 2: *That's my problem. I just have to CARE enough.* (Tries to rub, pat, jump, and bend all at once again while mumbling.) *I care, I care, I care.*

PONDER: (Laughs and shakes head.) *It's going to take a lot more than caring for you to do those four things all at once. Let's go and find something else to do.* (Exit together.)

BP23: Doing Okay?

Cast: Ponder the Frog, Noah's Park Puppet 2

Note: If your Puppet 2 is Stretch, change the name in the script to another Noah's Park puppet.

Ponder is onstage.

PUPPET 2: *(Enters.)* **Hey, Ponder, do you think Howler is doing okay?**

PONDER: **Yes.**

PUPPET 2: **Are you sure?**

PONDER: **Yes, I saw him just a little bit ago.**

PUPPET 2: **Do you think Stretch is doing okay?**

PONDER: **Yes.**

PUPPET 2: **Are you sure? She's not lost or anything?**

PONDER: **I'm sure.**

PUPPET 2: **Do you think Jesus is doing okay?**

PONDER: *(Looks back and forth between Puppet 2 and audience.)* **Why are you asking all these questions,** *(Name of Puppet 2)***?**

PUPPET 2: **Just wondering. Do you know that Jesus loves us and has done so many good things for us?**

PONDER: **Yes, I know that. But why are you worried about all your friends? What is this about?**

PUPPET 2: *I want to make sure that the people who love me are okay—and Jesus too, because He loves me. I like being loved and talking to people I love. So, I just thought I'd check. Are you sure you're okay?*

PONDER: *I'm sure. But,* (Name of Puppet 2)*, I think you're doing a lot of unnecessary work.*

PUPPET 2: *What do you mean?*

PONDER: *You really don't have to always go around checking up on everyone. Jesus loves all these people you love, so He's watching out for them.*

PUPPET 2: *Jesus loves all these people that I love?*

PONDER: *Yes, He does. He loves them and He does good things for them.*

PUPPET 2: *What a relief! Well, I've got to go now.*

PONDER: *But you just got here.*

PUPPET 2: *I know, but I'm going to go and see just HOW Jesus is loving all of the people I love.*

PONDER: *Well, okay. I'll see you later.* (Puppet 2 exits. Ponder turns to the kids.) *In case you're wondering, Jesus IS okay, and He loves each of you too!*

BP24: Serving with Love

Cast: Ponder the Frog, Noah's Park Puppet 2

Props: A puppet-size tray

Puppet 2 is holding a tray, standing by Ponder.

PUPPET 2: *(Holds tray up high.)* **Is this how you hold the tray when you're a server in a restaurant?**

PONDER: *Only if you're a waiter on T.V. Hold it at your waist.*

PUPPET 2: *I can't hold it there with only one hand.*

PONDER: *You're not supposed to hold it with only one hand. You're supposed to hold it with two hands.*

PUPPET 2: *Are you sure?*

PONDER: *Yes, that's how a server brings food to people in restaurants.*

PUPPET 2: *When do the servers get to sit down?*

PONDER: *When they're done working.*

PUPPET 2: *How long do they work. A minute? Ten minutes? An hour?*

PONDER: *A lot of hours.*

PUPPET 2: *There are people who bring other people food, and they don't get to sit down for hours?*

PONDER: *That's right. Waiters and waitresses must be nice to everyone and help those they are serving.*

PUPPET 2: *That's a lot of work!*

PONDER: *It is, but they get trained for it, just as Jesus teaches US to serve.*

PUPPET 2: *This serving stuff is hard.*

PONDER: *Sometimes it can be very hard. Learning how Jesus wants us to serve is sometimes easier because He also teaches us how to love each other. If you LOVE someone, it's often easier to serve them.*

PUPPET 2: *That makes sense. But Jesus doesn't make us hold trays of food if we're not any good at it, does he?*

PONDER: *Not usually.*

PUPPET 2: *Good. (Drops the tray with a crash.) I'll find another way to serve.*

PONDER: *That sounds good, (Name of Puppet 2). Let's go to over to Cozy Cave and see if anyone there needs our help.*

PUPPET 2: *Okay.*

(Exit together.)

BP25: Getting to the Bottom of Forgiveness

Cast: Ponder the Frog, Noah's Park Puppet 2

Props: A self-adhesive bandage

Ponder and Puppet 2 are onstage. Puppet 2 has a bandage on its head.

PUPPET 2: *Ow! Ow! When is this going to stop hurting?*

PONDER: *What happened to you?*

PUPPET 2: *I was hurrying to Polka Dot Pond for a drink of water, and I fell down and skinned my elbow.*

PONDER: *That sounds painful.*

PUPPET 2: *It was. It hurt so much. But you know what hurt even worse?*

PONDER: *No, what?*

PUPPET 2: *All my friends were there. Instead of helping me up, they laughed.*

PONDER: *Why would they do that?*

PUPPET 2: *They're mean, awful animals, and I'll never forgive them!*

PONDER: *If you never forgive your friends, you'll have no one to play with or talk to or hang out with. Is that really what you want?*

PUPPET 2: (Thinks.) *No.*

PONDER: *Then you'd better forgive them. They were wrong to do that. Have you every hurt someone's feelings?*

PUPPET 2: *I suppose so.*

PONDER: *Remember how Jesus forgave everyone? He forgave people even though He never disobeyed God, even once.*

PUPPET 2: *You're right. I'll forgive my friends for laughing at me.*

PONDER: *It does bother me, though, that all the animals would stand there and laugh at you instead of helping you or being sad for you.*

PUPPET 2: *Well, I guess it was a little funny.*

PONDER: *Falling was funny?*

PUPPET 2: *Well . . . I found a ballerina tutu, and I put it on and was pretending to dance with a coconut shell on my head. And everything was going fine until I slipped on a banana peel and couldn't keep my balance. I grabbed at Howler's mane, and pulled him down as I was falling into Ivory who tried to keep me up, but she toppled over too . . .*

PONDER: *(Chuckles.)* **So, you weren't the only one who fell.**

PUPPET 2: *No, I was on the bottom of the pile. It **WAS** kind of funny. (Exit laughing.)*

BP26: Need Help Out of the Hole?

Cast: Ponder the Frog, Noah's Park Puppet 2

Puppet 2 is onstage but is sunk below the stage so the kids can see only its head and one hand.

PUPPET 2: *Help! Help me! Is anyone there? I need help! Help!*

PONDER: *(Enters.) (Name of Puppet 2)? There you are. What happened?*

PUPPET 2: *I fell into this hole. It's so deep that I don't know how to get out of it.*

PONDER: *That is deep. Here, give me your hands. (Both Puppets hold hands and slowly Ponder pulls Puppet 2 out of the hole.)*

PUPPET 2: *Thank you, Ponder. (Hugs Ponder.) Thank you so much! I thought I was going to be in there forever!*

PONDER: *No one heard you calling?*

PUPPET 2: *No one until you.*

PONDER: *I'm glad that God isn't like that. Jesus teaches us to ask God for help.*

PUPPET 2: *That's great to know.*

PONDER: *It is, because sometimes it feels like you've fallen in a hole.*

PUPPET 2: *Like when you're sad that a friend is moving away? Or when someone gets a bigger piece of cake than you do? Or when you have to clean your bedroom all by yourself?*

PONDER: *Or when something bad happens to someone you know.*

PUPPET 2: *Or someone gets you in trouble. Or you get sick.*

PONDER: *There are a lot of times when you feel like you're in a hole and can't get out, even though you're not really in a dirt hole.*

PUPPET 2: *When you're in these pretend holes, should you cry out for help?*

PONDER: *Definitely. A lot of times kids do cry out but no one seems to hear them. That's when they need to know that they should ask God for help. Sometimes, only He can help them out of the hole. Or He sends someone to help.*

PUPPET 2: *Holes are a scary place to be.*

PONDER: *They are. But don't ever forget, if you ask God for help . . .*

PONDER & PUPPET 2: *God will always hear you.*

PONDER: *Let's go get that dirt brushed off of you. I'll help!*

(Exit together.)

BP27: Easy Questions

Cast: Ponder the Frog, Noah's Park Puppet 2

Ponder is onstage.

PUPPET 2: *(Enters.)* **Ponder, how do you know that the sun will rise?**

PONDER: **Because it rises every morning, whether the clouds block it from our view or not.**

PUPPET 2: **How do you know that rain is made out of water?**

PONDER: **Because the rain falls into my pond and is no different than the other water already in the pond.**

PUPPET 2: **How do you know that you can't touch a rainbow?**

PONDER: **Because I've never met anyone who has.** *(Name of Puppet 2)*, **why are you asking me all these questions?**

PUPPET 2: **I wanted to help you.**

PONDER: **How does asking questions help me?**

PUPPET 2: **Well, I started by asking you easy questions . . .**

PONDER: **Those were easy?**

PUPPET 2: **Very easy compared to what I want to ask you. I'm trying to lead up to a very hard question.**

PONDER: *You're making me worried,* (Name of Puppet 2). *Just ask me the HARD question. I can't take any more of your EASY questions.*

PUPPET 2: (Puppet 2 massages Ponders shoulders.) *Are you sure you're ready?*

PONDER: (Pats Puppet 2 on the back reassuringly.) *I'm ready.*

PUPPET 2: *Okay. Here goes: How do you know that Jesus is God's Son?*

PONDER: (Laughs.) *That's an easy question! Give me a harder one.*

PUPPET 2: *Easy! How is it easy? If it's so easy, what's the answer?*

PONDER: *I know that Jesus is God's Son because God raised Him from the dead. It says so in the Bible.*

PUPPET 2: *Oh, of course, the Bible! And we can trust God's special Book, so Jesus must be God's Son. Hmmm, I guess that IS rather easy, isn't it? Well then, what about my other questions. Does the Bible tell us anything about the sun, rain, or rainbows?*

PONDER: (Laughs.) *As a matter of fact, it does! Let's go have a look in my Bible.*

(Exit arm in arm.)

BP28: Even Bigger

Cast: Ponder the Frog, Noah's Park Puppet 2

Puppet 2 is onstage.

PUPPET 2: *Hey, kids! Welcome to a new game show called "Even Bigger." I'm your host,* (Name of Puppet 2). *In this show, a player will build on each word I say, telling about something that God gave us. The challenge is to come up with something even bigger that God gave us than what was just said. And now, please help me welcome our first and only player, Ponder the Frog!* (Leads the children in clapping.)

PONDER: (Enters.) *Hi, I'm glad to be here on your game show.*

PUPPET 2: *Ponder, are you ready to play "Even Bigger"?*

PONDER: *I'm ready.*

PUPPET 2: *Okay, here we go. I'll start the game by saying "seeds." Now you must come up with something that God gives us that is even bigger than seeds.*

PONDER: *Grass.*

PUPPET 2: *Very good. Now, I have to find something bigger than grass that God has given us. Hmmm. How* *about flowers?*

PONDER: *Good. Then I'll say trees.*

PUPPET 2: *That's bigger. Hmmm, how about rocks? Rocks can be bigger than trees.*

PONDER: *And mountains are bigger than rocks.*

PUPPET 2: *Continents are bigger than mountains.*

PONDER: *Oceans are even bigger.*

PUPPET 2: *The world is bigger than all the oceans.*

PONDER: *The sun is bigger than the world.*

PUPPET 2: *The solar system.*

PONDER: *The whole universe!*

PUPPET 2: (Pauses.) *I know what's even bigger— the truth that Jesus prays for us!*

PONDER: *That's big. Real big, but I know something that God gave us that was even bigger. He gave us His Son.*

PUPPET 2: *And we have a winner! Nothing, absolutely nothing, is bigger than that.*

PONDER: *What do I win?*

PUPPET 2: *God's already given you His Son. We can't give you anything bigger than that!* (Exit.)

BP29: The Masked Superhero

Cast: Ponder the Frog, Noah's Park Puppet 2

Props: A puppet-size mask and cape

Ponder is onstage.

PUPPET 2: *(Leaps onstage, wearing a mask and cape; pretends to fly around the stage once.)* **Never fear! Your Masked Superhero is here!** *(Stops by Ponder, panting.)*

PONDER: **What do you do, Masked Superhero?**

PUPPET 2: **I use my superhero power to help you.**

PONDER: **Can you make more bugs so that I have more to eat?**

PUPPET 2: **No.**

PONDER: **Can you make more lily pads for me to hop on?**

PUPPET 2: **No.**

PONDER: **Can you make the sky rain to cool off a hot day?**

PUPPET 2: **No.**

PONDER: **Can you make me well if I get sick?**

PUPPET 2: **Don't be silly, Ponder.**

PONDER: **Well, Masked Superhero, what DO you do?**

PUPPET 2: *I have a mask and a cape, and I fly around the world!*

PONDER: *How does that help me?*

PUPPET 2: *Ponder, you're ruining my game.*

PONDER: *I'm sorry, but I don't understand the point of your superhero powers. If it's all the same to you, I'm going to keep Jesus as my favorite superhero.*

PUPPET 2: *Jesus isn't a superhero.*

PONDER: *He is to me. His powers are real, and He uses them to help us.*

PUPPET 2: *You can't compare me to Jesus. I'm just playing a game, and He's for real.*

PONDER: *That's true. Okay. I'll play along. Quick, Masked Superhero, go fly somewhere.*

PUPPET 2: *I'm on my way!* (Puppet 2 pretends to fly away.)

BP30: Hurray for the King!

Cast: Ponder the Frog, Noah's Park Puppet 2

Ponder and Puppet 2 are onstage.

PUPPET 2: *Thanks for helping me practice, Ponder. I'm so nervous.*

PONDER: *It's my pleasure. Okay, kids,* (Name of Puppet 2) *is going to go offstage. When* (Name of Puppet 2) *comes back, everyone needs to clap and shout, "Hurray! Hurray! Yea for* (Name of Puppet 2)*!"*

PUPPET 2: *Okay, I'm leaving now.* (Exits, then calls from offstage.) *Are you ready?*

PONDER: *We're ready.*

PUPPET 2: *Here I come.* (Enters.)

PONDER: (Claps hands.) *Hurray! Hurray! Yea for* (Name of Puppet 2)*!*

PUPPET 2: *That was pretty good. Can we try it again?*

PONDER: *Sure.*

PUPPET 2: *Okay, I'm leaving now.* (Exits.) *Are you ready?*

PONDER: *We're ready. Kids, let's be really loud this time, okay?*

PUPPET 2: *Here I come.* (Enters.)

PONDER: *(Claps hands.)* **Hurray! Hurray! Yea for** *(Name of Puppet 2)***!**

PUPPET 2: *I think I get it now. Is that how the people in Jerusalem treated Jesus?*

PONDER: *Yes, they yelled for Him and called Him their King.*

PUPPET 2: *Wow! If these kids here can make this much noise, just imagine how much noise all the people along the street made yelling for Jesus.*

PONDER: *Praising Jesus did not end back in Bible times. Did you know that we can still praise Jesus as our King?*

PUPPET 2: *We can? How can we do that?*

PONDER: *Let's all clap our hands and yell, "Hurray! Hurray! Yea for Jesus, our King!"*

PUPPET 2: *Okay, kids, are you ready?*

PONDER: *One, two, three. (Claps.) "Hurray! Hurray! Yea for Jesus, our King!"*

PUPPET 2: *One more time! (Claps.) "Hurray! Hurray! Yea for Jesus, our King!"*

PONDER: *You did great, kids!*

(Exit, clapping.)

BP31: The Lost Voice

Cast: Ponder the Frog, Noah's Park Puppet 2

Ponder is onstage. Puppet 2 enters.

PUPPET 2: *I want to sing a song, but I don't want to sing it alone. Ponder, will you sing it with me?*

PONDER: *(Speaks in a stage whisper.)* **I'd love to, but I lost my voice.**

PUPPET 2: *What did you say, Ponder? I can't hear you.*

PONDER: *(Speaks hoarsely.)* **I lost my voice.**

PUPPET 2: *Do you need me to help you find it?*

PONDER: *(Hoarse.)* **No, I didn't LOSE it somewhere. My voice isn't WORKing.**

PUPPET 2: *Oh! Do you mean you've got a FROG in your throat? (Puppet 2 snickers. Ponder shakes his head sadly.) I just had to say that. But, Ponder, will your voice ever get better?*

PONDER: *(Hoarse.)* **It'll get better.**

PUPPET 2: *That's kind of like how the sun goes down, and it gets dark. I think it will be dark forever, but the next morning the sun comes back up. Your voice has gone away, and it will come back.*

PONDER: *(Hoarse.)* **Something like that.**

PUPPET 2: *(Speaking with poetic drama.)* **Or like a flower that dies in the fall, but part of it stays underground all winter. Then in the spring it comes back to life.**

PONDER: *(Hoarse.)* **That might be stretching it a little.**

PUPPET 2: *(Speaking with dramatic excitement.)* **Or like Jesus when He died and then came back to life after three days.**

PONDER: *(Hoarse.)* **Don't get carried away. My voice will come back in a few days because that's the way God made my voice.**

PUPPET 2: **God has given us such a wonderful world. The sun rises every morning. Flowers bloom in the spring. Jesus is alive. And you're going to get your voice back.**

PONDER: *(Hoarse.)* **God did an excellent job.**

PUPPET 2: **He sure did. That just makes me want to sing! Since you can't sing with me, Ponder, maybe the kids will sing a song with me.** *(Have Puppet 2 lead the kids in a song they know well that celebrates Jesus' being alive.)*

BP32: The Hidden Forest

Cast: Ponder the Frog, Noah's Park Puppet 2

Props: A few leaves and twigs scattered about the stage

Ponder and Puppet 2 slowly walk along beside each other.

PUPPET 2: *(Points around the stage.)* **This is the ugliest field I've ever seen.**

PONDER: **It used to be a forest.**

PUPPET 2: **A forest? That's impossible. It's a black field. There aren't any trees with big green leaves. There are only a few black trunks.**

PONDER: **There was a fire here last year. I think your family was away when it happened. Fortunately, no one was hurt at the time.**

PUPPET 2: **A fire? I do remember something about a fire. Fires sure make things look bad. There's nothing to eat in a forest that's been burned.**

PONDER: **True.**

PUPPET 2: **Okay, what do I need to do?** *(Puppet 2 rubs its hands together and looks around as if getting ready to work.)*

PONDER: **What do you mean?**

PUPPET 2: **There was a fire here where there used to be plants. We need more plants here. What should I do?**

PONDER: **What are you asking?**

PUPPET 2: *Ponder, the forest needs trees, bushes, grasses, and vines. It needs plants. How can I make plants?*

PONDER: *Do you have any seeds?*

PUPPET 2: *No. I want to make plants, not play with seeds.*

PONDER: *Only God can make plants.*

PUPPET 2: *What? Well, He needs to make some here. There are no plants.*

PONDER: *You're not looking closely enough.* (Ponder lifts a leaf from the ground.) **God has been working all year. Look.**

PUPPET 2: *It's a bunch of tiny plants!*

PONDER: (Leads Puppet 2 across the stage.) **And look over here.** (Moves some twigs.)

PUPPET 2: *There's a small tree starting to grow!*

PONDER: *We can plant seeds that God has already made. But only God can make plants.*

PUPPET 2: *That is amazing! From far away, the forest looks all black. But up close, I can see that God has been working. Maybe there's a whole forest hiding underneath this burnt ground!*

PONDER: (Laughs.) **Yes,** (Name of Puppet 2). **And only God can make—or hide—a forest!**

BP33: All Those Animals

Cast: Ponder the Frog, Noah's Park Puppet 2

Ponder and Puppet 2 are onstage.

PUPPET 2: *Ponder, do you know where the best clay is?*

PONDER: *No, where is it?*

PUPPET 2: *I don't know. I was asking you. I know that sometimes you can find clay under the water. Sand and silt have heavier minerals in them than clay does, so clay often settles on top of them.*

PONDER: *What do you need clay for?*

PUPPET 2: *I'm going to make clay statues of all of my friends.*

PONDER: *Can you do that?*

PUPPET 2: *Of course! I'm going to make a camel, rhinoceros, giraffe, frog, monkey, raccoon, lion, elephant, and dove.*

PONDER: *You sound like you're going to have as much fun as God did.*

PUPPET 2: *What do you mean?*

PONDER: *Just think about how much fun God must have had when He made all the animals. He made a hump on camels to make them special. He* *gave the rhinoceroses horns to make them special. He gave giraffes long necks, frogs strong legs, monkeys useful tails, raccoons masks, lions manes, elephants trunks, and doves wings.*

PUPPET 2: *What an imagination God must have!*

PONDER: *You're right! And He didn't stop with just the kinds of animals that are your friends here in the park.*

PUPPET 2: *Do you mean there are more?*

PONDER: *Yes, God also made animals like the Blue-Ringed Octopus, the Long-Nosed Potoroo, the Four-Toed Jerboa, the African Spur-Thighed Tortoise, and cute Sugar Gliders.*

PUPPET 2: *Wow.*

PONDER: *God made so many different things that we couldn't even name them all.*

PUPPET 2: *I don't even want to try. I want to make my clay statues.*

PONDER: *Let's go over to Polka Dot Pond and try to find some clay for you.*

PUPPET 2: *That sounds great! Do you want to make a statue, too?*

PONDER: *No, I want to cool off. It's hot today.* (Exit together.)

BP34: The Special Secret Something

Cast: Ponder the Frog, Noah's Park Puppet 2, Leader or Park Patrol actor

Ponder and Puppet 2 are onstage. Leader stands by them.

PUPPET 2: *(To Leader.)* **Let's see. You have a nose, and I have a nose.** *(Both touch their noses.)*

LEADER: **And we both have eyes.**

PUPPET 2: **Two of them. And we both use our ears to hear.**

LEADER: **That's true. We both use our legs to walk.**

PUPPET 2: **Or run. We're a lot alike.**

PONDER: **But animals and people are different, too.**

PUPPET 2: **That's true. We eat different foods, and we live in different places.**

PONDER: **Those are differences, but there's an even bigger difference. God made people very special.**

PUPPET 2: **Did God add a special secret something to people that He didn't add to animals?**

PONDER: **Yes, He did.**

LEADER: **That's right. God made people in**

His likeness—to be like Him.

PUPPET 2: And that's what makes people extra special?

LEADER: Yes, God gave people very special gifts and abilities.

PUPPET 2: Do all people have these gifts and abilities, even these kids?

PONDER: Yes, every child born and every grown adult has these special gifts from God.

PUPPET 2: What do people do with their special gifts?

PONDER: They can use them to learn who God is.

PUPPET 2: Wow! That's a really special gift. (Puppet 2 breathes loudly on Leader.)

LEADER: What are you doing?

PUPPET 2: (Breathes on Leader again.) Do you feel any special gifts or abilities?

LEADER: (Waves hand in front of face.) The only thing I feel is your stinky breath! (Pats Puppet 2 on back.) You're a good friend and a great animal, (name of Puppet 2), but you definitely can't do what God can do.

BP35: A Caring Leader

Cast: Ponder the Frog, Noah's Park Puppet 2, Leader or Park Patrol actor

Props: A small book

Note: If the part of Leader is played by a male, change the appropriate pronouns in the skit. If the puppet you are using for Puppet 2 is named in the skit, substitute the name of another Noah's Park puppet in that place.

Leader is in front of the stage. Puppet 2 carries a book onstage.

LEADER: *Hey, (Name of Puppet 2), **let me help you with that.***

PUPPET 2: *Thanks, (Name of Leader).*

LEADER: *No problem.*

PUPPET 2: *I need to put it on the table over there.*

LEADER: *Then I'll walk over to the table and put it down for you. (Takes book from Puppet 2.)*

PONDER: *(Enters.) (Name of Leader), **thanks for waking up Dreamer and talking to Screech about not playing jokes on Honk.***

LEADER: *No problem. I've got to go now, but if you see Howler, tell him that I found his comb, and tell Ivory that there's a ripe blueberry bush on the*

south side of Polka Dot Pond.

PONDER: *Okay, I will.* (Leader exits with book.)

PUPPET 2: (Name of Leader) *is sure a busy person.*

PONDER: *Yes, she is. She takes good care of us animals and the wonderful world that God has given her.*

PUPPET 2: *The whole world belongs to* (Name of Leader)*?*

PONDER: *No, no. What I meant was that God made people special, and they take care of the world.*

PUPPET 2: *Is that why* (Name of Leader) *does things for us and helps us out?*

PONDER: *I think that's part of it.*

PUPPET 2: *Is there another reason too?*

PONDER: *I think so.*

PUPPET 2: *What is it?*

PONDER: (Name of Leader) *takes care of us because God asked her to take care of His world, but I also think that she helps us out because she likes us.*

PUPPET 2: *That makes sense. I like her, too. Let's go tell Ivory and Howler what* (Name of Leader) *said.*

PONDER: *Good idea.*

(Exit together.)

BP36: The Family God Gave You

Cast: Ponder the Frog, Noah's Park Puppet 2

Ponder and Puppet 2 are onstage.

PUPPET 2: *That's it! I'm running away from home.*

PONDER: *You're running away? What happened,* (Name of Puppet 2)*?*

PUPPET 2: *I'm not appreciated.*

PONDER: *Not appreciated for what?*

PUPPET 2: *I'm not appreciated for who I am. I feel like a servant who has to do what everyone else in my family wants me to do. My mother wants me to clean up all the time. My father wants me to go with him to learn survival skills. My brother needs me to help him play games. My sister is always complaining that I'm not doing things exactly right. I'm running away to make a new start.*

PONDER: *Where are you going to live?*

PUPPET 2: *(Thinks.) Uh, I don't know.*

PONDER: *What are you going to eat?*

PUPPET 2: *(Thinks.) I don't know.*

PONDER: *Where will you find water?*

PUPPET 2: *(Thinks.) I don't know.*

PONDER: *Who will be your friends?*

PUPPET 2: *I don't know. (Puppet 2 starts to cry.)* *Running away from home is so much more complicated than I thought it was going to be.*

PONDER: *(Comforts Puppet 2.)* **Don't cry,** *(Name of Puppet 2).* **I care about what will happen to you, and God cares too. He cares about where you live, what you eat, and what happens to you. And, you'll be happy to know, your family cares too.**

PUPPET 2: *What is going to happen to me?* *(Puppet 2 cries again.)*

PONDER: *If you run away, I don't know. If you learn to work through your problems at home, I think you'll be okay. You have parents, a brother, and a sister who all care for you.*

PUPPET 2: *(Sniffling.) I miss my family already. What should I do, Ponder?*

PONDER: *God has given you a family. They may not be perfect, but they do care about you. Through them, God will help you get what you need to live.*

PUPPET 2: *You're right. I need my family. I need my parents. I need the home that God gave me. (Turns to leave.)* **Mommy! Daddy!** *(Exits.)*

BP37: Friendly Ways

Cast: Ponder the Frog, Noah's Park Puppet 2

Props: Telephone

Puppet 2 is talking into the telephone. Ponder is talking to the kids.

PUPPET 2: *I don't know. What do you like to do?*

PONDER: **See kids,** *(Name of Puppet 2)* **is being a friend. Instead of telling his friend what he wants to do, he is asking what his friend likes to do.**

PUPPET 2: *(Laughs.)* **That is such a funny story. You're a good storyteller.**

PONDER: **Now** *(Name of Puppet 2)* **is being a friend by listening and giving him a compliment.**

PUPPET 2: **Can I help you do that?**

PONDER: **Did you hear that, kids?** *(Name of Puppet 2)* **is finding a way to help his friend. That's a great way to be a friend.**

PUPPET 2: **I felt that way too. Then I decided to pray and ask God to help me.**

PONDER: **Sharing your faith with someone is another way to be a friend. It sounds like** *(Name of Puppet 2)* **is letting God be a part of his friendship.**

PUPPET 2: *Okay, then.* (Pauses as if listening.) **It was nice talking to you.** (Pauses.) **Okay, goodbye.** (Puppet 2 hangs up the telephone.)

PONDER: **Hello,** (Name of Puppet 2).

PUPPET 2: **Hi, Ponder. I didn't see you. I was talking on the telephone.**

PONDER: **I know. You were busy being a friend. You were looking out for your friend's best interests.**

PUPPET 2: **I was?**

PONDER: **Yes. You listened closely to what your friend had to say and tried to find a way to help him.**

PUPPET 2: **I did?**

PONDER: **But most importantly, you let God be a part of your friendship.**

PUPPET 2: **Are you sure?**

PONDER: (Laughs.) **Of course. I heard you talking. Who were you talking to?**

PUPPET 2: **I don't know.**

PONDER: **What do you mean, you don't know?**

PUPPET 2: **I mean I don't know. It was a wrong number.**

PONDER: **Oh no! Kids, don't ever try that at home!**

(Exit.)

BP38: Counting Fears Away

Cast: Ponder the Frog, Noah's Park Puppet 2, someone to work the lights

Props: Something to make thunder noises (such as banging on a metal cabinet)

Ponder and Puppet 2 are huddled together. Lights switch on and off like lightning; loud thunder noises are heard.

PUPPET 2: *This is a terrible storm! It's raining so hard out there.*

PONDER: *It's a good thing we have Cozy Cave to wait in.*

PUPPET 2: *I don't mind the rain, but the thunder and lightning scare me.* (Large thunder sound.) **Yikes!** (Puppet 2 holds Ponder tighter.)

PONDER: *Don't be afraid.* (Large thunder sound.)

PUPPET 2: *Yikes!*

PONDER: *God can help us through this.*

PUPPET 2: *If you say so.*

PONDER: *I do say so. Polka Dot Pond was getting pretty shallow. We need this rain to fill it back up again.*

PUPPET 2: *Like I said, I don't mind the rain.*

PONDER: *And thunder and lightning just happen when there's a rainstorm.*

PUPPET 2: *Maybe, but they still scare me.*

PONDER: *Let's play a game.*

PUPPET 2: *Okay.*

PONDER: *The next time we see lightning, let's count: 1001, 1002, 1003, and so on until we hear the thunder. Then we'll know how far away the lightning is. Look! There's lightning. Let's count.*

PONDER & PUPPET 2: *1001, 1002, 1003, 1004, 1005, 1006, 1007*
(Thunder crashes.)

PUPPET 2: *That means that the lightning is 1007 miles away?*

PONDER: *No, it means that the lightning is seven miles away.*

PUPPET 2: *That's pretty far. There's more lightning!*

PONDER & PUPPET 2: *1001, 1002, 1003, 1004, 1005, 1006, 1007, 1008*
(Thunder crashes.)

PUPPET 2: *That lightning was eight miles away. That's not so scary.*

PONDER: *God made thunder and lightning for a purpose, but not to scare you.*

PUPPET 2: *And I feel less afraid now. I'm glad God sent you to help me, Ponder.*

BP39: Prickly Rules

Cast: Ponder the Frog, Noah's Park Puppet 2

Props: Small branches

Ponder and Puppet 2 are on one side of the stage. The branches are piled on the other side to represent the sticker patch.

PUPPET 2: *(Bragging to the kids.)* **I don't like rules. "Do this. Do that." Well, I don't have to if I don't want to.**

PONDER: **Be careful,** *(Puppet 2).*

PUPPET 2: *(Ignores Ponder. To kids.)* **"Be careful"— there's another rule! But I can do what I want. I can go where I choose. Everyone tells me, "Stay out of the sticker patch." But if I want to go in the sticker patch, I'll go in the sticker patch.** *(Points to the sticker patch.)*

PONDER: *(Name of Puppet 2),* **why do you think that your parents tell you to stay out of that sticker patch?**

PUPPET 2: *(Turns to Ponder.)* **Because they're mean.**

PONDER: *(Chuckles.)* **No, that's not the reason.**

PUPPET 2: **That's how little you know. I don't need rules. If I want to go into the sticker patch, I will go into the sticker patch.**

PONDER: **I wouldn't if I were you.**

PUPPET 2: *Well, you're not me.*

PONDER: *(Sighs.)* **Don't do it.**

PUPPET 2: *(Puppet 2 moves behind the branches to appear to be in them. Talks to kids.)* **Now I am in the sticker patch because I WANT to be in the sticker patch.**

PONDER: **No one WANTS to be in a sticker patch.**

PUPPET 2: *(Turns to look at Ponder.)* **I do. I . . . ouch. Ow.** *(Keeps pulling an arm back or trying to jump away from a prickle.)* **That hurts. Ouch. Ow. Oh. Ouch. Oooo!** *(Puppet 2 runs out of the sticker patch.)* **Ow. Ow. Those stickers hurt.**

PONDER: **That's why your parents told you to stay out of the sticker patch.**

PUPPET 2: **I thought they wanted to keep good things from me.**

PONDER: **Oh, no. Your parents want to protect you from things that will hurt you. God gives us rules for the same reason. He wants us to have what we need and doesn't want anything to hurt us.**

PUPPET 2: **I've never thought of rules like that. Ponder, could you help me take all these stickers off of me?**

PONDER: **Sure. Come over here where there's more light.** *(Exit together.)*

BP40: A Sweet Present

Cast: Ponder the Frog, Noah's Park Puppet 2

Props: A piece of candy

PUPPET 2:	*(Runs back and forth across the stage.)* **I need candy! Candy! Does anyone have any candy for me? I'll die if I don't get some candy!**
PONDER:	*(Enters with candy.)* **Hello,** *(Name of Puppet 2)*.
PUPPET 2:	**Candy! You have candy! Give it to me quick!**
PONDER:	**What?**
PUPPET 2:	**Your piece of candy! I need your piece of candy. Give it to me!**
PONDER:	*(Name of Puppet 2)*, **you're being rude.**
PUPPET 2:	**I am not. How can you say that? Don't you see I'm desperate? I need a piece of candy!**
PONDER:	**You don't NEED candy.**
PUPPET 2:	**My hands are shaking, and my ears are twitching. How can you be so mean?**
PONDER:	*(Name of Puppet 2)*, **there's a difference between needing and wanting. You WANT candy. You don't NEED it.**
PUPPET 2:	**How do you know?**

PONDER: *God knows what you need. Through your parents, God has given you love, food, and a place to live.*

PUPPET 2: *But the food they give me isn't candy.*

PONDER: *I hope not! Your parents love you like God does. They know that if you eat too much candy, you won't be able to grow up strong and healthy. You don't need candy. You just want it.*

PUPPET 2: *Well, maybe I don't need it, but I want it a lot.*

PONDER: *That I can believe.*

PUPPET 2: *Who are you going to give that candy to? Are you going to eat it?*

PONDER: *No. I got this piece of candy for a friend of mine.*

PUPPET 2: *You must like your friend a lot.*

PONDER: *I do. He's very special.*

PUPPET 2: *I hope your friend likes it.*

PONDER: *I'm sure he will. (Name of Puppet 2), I got it for . . . YOU!*

PUPPET 2: *For me? You got that piece of candy for me? (Hugs Ponder.) You're such a great friend! Thank you, Ponder. Thank you, thank you! (Exit.)*

BP41: Be Yourself

Cast: Ponder the Frog, Noah's Park Puppet 2

Ponder is onstage. Puppet 2 rushes on.

PUPPET 2: *Ponder, I need your advice! I want to become friends with that new animal at the water hole. But how should I talk to him?*

PONDER: *Just be yourself.*

PUPPET 2: *That's not a good answer. Hmmm, maybe I won't say anything for a while and make HIM really want to talk to ME.*

PONDER: *Not talking to someone doesn't make a good friend.*

PUPPET 2: *And talking does?*

PONDER: *Yes, it does.*

PUPPET 2: *Then I'll introduce myself and I'll talk a lot. I'll tell him everything I know and talk so fast that we'll become the best of friends.*

PONDER: *Hold on,* (Name of Puppet 2). *Talking without listening doesn't make a good friend either.*

PUPPET 2: *So, I have to talk AND I have to listen? This is complicated. I wish friendship came with directions!*

PONDER: *Jesus' helpers felt the same way. So,*

> Jesus gave them the Lord's Prayer as a pattern for a way that people could talk to God.

PUPPET 2: *That was nice of Him.*

PONDER: *Yes it was. Jesus wanted people to pray to God—because God is our friend, our teacher, our helper, the one who takes care of us, and many other things. God loves us that much.*

PUPPET 2: *So "pray" means to talk to God?*

PONDER: *That's right. God loves people and wants them to talk AND listen to Him.*

PUPPET 2: *Just as I want to talk AND listen to the new animal at the water hole?*

PONDER: *Exactly.*

PUPPET 2: *So what should I say?*

PONDER: *(Throws up his hands.)* **Introduce yourself—**

PUPPET 2: *I can do that.*

PONDER: *—And then be yourself.*

> *(Puppet 2 nods and then exits with Ponder.)*

BP42: God and Me

Cast: Ponder the Frog, Noah's Park Puppet 2

Props: A small, red, helium balloon with string or yarn

Ponder is onstage. Puppet 2 enters with balloon tied to its wrist

PONDER:	*What a nice balloon, (Name of Puppet 2).*
PUPPET 2:	*What balloon?*
PONDER:	*The balloon floating above your head.*
PUPPET 2:	*(Laughs) I forgot that I had a balloon. Flutter found this balloon floating in the sky. She brought it down to me because it's red, and she knows that red is my favorite color. Then I tied it to my arm.*
PONDER:	*How long ago was that?*
PUPPET 2:	*Yesterday.*
PONDER:	*Yesterday?*
PUPPET 2:	*Yeah. I played with it all day. Then when I fell asleep, I forgot all about it. I guess it's been following me around all day.*
PONDER:	*And you never noticed it?*
PUPPET 2:	*Nope.*
PONDER:	*That's often how we treat God. He's*

with us wherever we go, but we
never seem to notice Him.

PUPPET 2: No way! If God were following me
around, I'd notice Him.

PONDER: God's been following you around all
your life, and that's a lot longer
than your balloon's been following
you.

PUPPET 2: Really? *(Ponder nods.)* **So God knows
everything that I do?** *(Ponder nods.)*
Does He also go everywhere that
every one of the kids in this room
goes?

PONDER: Yes, He does. God loves each person
in this room very much. He'll be
with them no matter where they go.

PUPPET 2: My balloon has been going
everywhere with me. Does that
mean that my balloon loves me too?

PONDER: No, your balloon follows you around
because you tied it to your arm. If
you cut the string, it would float
away.

PUPPET 2: Will God float away, too, someday?

PONDER: No, God will always be there. He
knows how to do the impossible.

PUPPET 2: Cool. *(Both exit.)*

BP43: The Achoo Rule

Cast: Ponder the Frog, Noah's Park Puppet 2

Props: A tissue

Puppet 2 is onstage holding a tissue. Ponder enters.

PUPPET 2: *A-a-a-choo! (Sniffles.)*

PONDER: *You sound like you've caught a cold, (Name of Puppet 2).*

PUPPET 2: *I did. Achoo!*

PONDER: *You didn't seem sick when I saw you yesterday. Did you catch it last night?*

PUPPET 2: *Yes. I ate candy all day instead of real food. I played out in the cold rain without my coat or boots—I got soaked! But I was having too much fun to come in. Then I stayed up real late last night. Achoo!*

PONDER: *That wasn't very smart.*

PUPPET 2: *That's what my mother said. She told me I'd catch a cold if I didn't eat healthy food and get plenty of rest and take care of myself.*

PONDER: *Did you listen?*

PUPPET 2: *No. She said . . . A-a-a-choo! (Sniffles.) She said that rules were made to help keep us safe and healthy, and that if I was going to* *break a rule, I would have to pay for it by catching a cold.*

PONDER: *So do you understand why your mother tells you to eat good food and get plenty of rest?*

PUPPET 2: *I . . . I—achoo–do.*

PONDER: *Your mother cares about your health and safety, just as God does. Your mother loves you very much, and so does God.*

PUPPET 2: *Then I'd better go home.*

PONDER: *Why?*

PUPPET 2: *My mother said that if I'm feeling sick that I should go home and get some more sleep.*

PONDER: *That's a good idea. And don't take the short cut by the crocodile canal. That wouldn't be safe either!*

PUPPET 2: *Thanks, Ponder, you're a good friend.*

PONDER: *I want you to get home safely too.*

BP44: Grateful Puppets

Cast: Ponder the Frog, Noah's Park Puppet 2

Ponder and Puppet 2 are onstage.

PUPPET 2: *(Looking up and around.)* **Thanks, God, for the sky. Thank You, God, for water. Thank You for trees. Thanks for clouds. Thank You, God, for grass. And God, thank You for my friends. Thank You for all the stars in the sky at night. Thank You, God, for my parents. Thank You for making me. Thank You for teaching the birds to sing. Thank You, God, for everything!**

PONDER: *What are you doing?*

PUPPET 2: **I'm thanking God.** *(Looks up again.)* **Thank You, God, for my legs. Thank You, God, for my eyes. Thanks for my ears. And thanks for my stomach.**

PONDER: *You're a very grateful animal today.*

PUPPET 2: **Yes, I am.** *(Looks up again.)* **Thanks for Ponder's legs and his eyes. Thank You for his ears and stomach.**

PONDER: *What you're doing—thanking God— is a really good thing. So don't misunderstand my question. But, why are you doing this?*

PUPPET 2: *Well, thanking God shows that we love Him.*

PONDER: *That's right.*

PUPPET 2: *So I wanted to show God that I love Him a who-o-o-le lot. I'm going to thank Him for everything I can see and everything I have.*

PONDER: *What a great idea. Would you like some help?*

PUPPET 2: *Sure.* (Looks up and around again.) *Thanks, God, for all that grass.*

PONDER: *Thank You, God, for lily pads.*

PUPPET 2: *Thank You for the bird that just flew over us.*

PONDER: *Thank You for my pond.*

PUPPET 2: *Thank You for Ponder wanting to thank You too.*

PONDER: (Both puppets walk toward side of stage as Ponder talks.) *Thank You, God, for Children's Church and all of the great kids who come to visit us every week.*

PUPPET 2: (Fading as they exit.) *And thank You for ice cream. That's a big one.*

BP45: Once Upon a Time

Cast: Ponder the Frog, Noah's Park Puppet 2

Props: A storybook

Puppet 2 is holding the book, standing by Ponder.

PUPPET 2: *Will you read me this storybook, Ponder?*

PONDER: *Sure,* (Name of Puppet 2).

PUPPET 2: *Oh, thank you so much. You've made me so happy!*

PONDER: (Laughs.) *Here, let me have it.* (Puppet 2 hands Ponder the book. Ponder opens it.) *Let's see, "Once upon a time . . ."*

PUPPET 2: *This is a great storybook. It's my favorite.*

PONDER: *I'm glad to hear that. I'll start reading now.*

PUPPET 2: *I can't wait.*

PONDER: *Once upon a time . . .*

PUPPET 2: *Have you ever read this story before?*

PONDER: *No, I haven't. Are you going to let me read it?*

PUPPET 2: *Oh yes. I love listening to this story.*

PONDER: *Once upon a time . . .*

PUPPET 2: *Do you like it so far? Isn't that the best beginning?*

PONDER: *(Puppet 2)*, **if you don't be quiet, I'm not going to read this to you.**

PUPPET 2: **I'll be quiet. You won't hear another word from me. Lock my lips and throw the key away.** *(Motions as if doing this.)*

PONDER: **Thank you.** *(Pauses and looks doubtfully at Puppet 2.)* **Once upon a time . . .**

PUPPET 2: **You won't even know I'm here.**

PONDER: **That's it. You take the book.** *(Hands Puppet 2 the book.)*

PUPPET 2: **But I want to hear the story!**

PONDER: **I'm sure you do. A lot of people say that about the Bible, too. They say they want to listen, but they just keep talking. You can listen to the story, just as people can listen to God's Word to show Him that they love Him. But you're not listening. You're talking. I can't read a story to you if you're talking!**

PUPPET 2: **Well, you don't have to get so upset. All I did was ask you to read me a story. If you didn't want to read it, all you had to do was say so.**

PONDER: **Aughhh!** *(Exits.)*

BP46: Blind Obedience

Cast: Ponder the Frog, Noah's Park Puppet 2

Props: Puppet-size blindfold

Puppet 2 is blindfolded and begins offstage. Ponder is onstage, talking to him.

PONDER: *(Calls to Puppet 2.)* **Okay,** *(Name of Puppet 2).* **Take two steps to your right.** *(There is the sound of a loud crash. Ponders hurries offstage.)* **To your right, not your left! Are you even listening to me?** *(Ponder returns, leading Puppet 2 by the hand.)*

PUPPET 2: **I WAS listening.**

PONDER: **I don't think so. First, I told you to walk straight, but you ran.**

PUPPET 2: **I thought I'd be able to get through the obstacle course quicker if I ran.**

PONDER: **Then I told you to duck, but you didn't. You walked right into a low-hanging tree limb.**

PUPPET 2: **I wish I had listened to you on that one. My head still hurts.**

PONDER: **Finally, I told you to take two steps to the right. You took two large hops to your left.**

PUPPET 2: **So maybe I'm not perfect.**

PONDER: *This isn't about being perfect. If you want me to give you directions, then you have to follow them. Otherwise, you might as well walk around with your blindfold all by yourself.*

PUPPET 2: *I'll get hurt if I do that.*

PONDER: *You won't get hurt any worse than you have with me. Not obeying is the same as doing it on your own.*

PUPPET 2: *I think you're overreacting a little.*

PONDER: *I'm not overreacting. When you obey, you show respect. It's like when we obey God. That's one way to show we love Him.*

PUPPET 2: *So, you don't think I love you?*

PONDER: *No, I don't think you know how to obey.*

PUPPET 2: *But I do.*

PONDER: *Then listen to what I say. Take two steps forward.*

PUPPET 2: *That's easy. One, two, three, four.* (Moves four steps and is offstage.)

PONDER: *TWO steps,* (Name of Puppet). ***Stop! Stop! You're going to hit that—***

PUPPET 2: *Ow!*

PONDER: *It would have been a lot less painful if you had obeyed. Here, let me help you again.* (Exits.)

BP47: The Choosy Robot

Cast: Ponder the Frog, Noah's Park Puppet 2

Ponder is onstage.

PUPPET 2: *(Enters, walking and talking like a robot. Speaks to Ponder.)* **What do you want me to do?**

PONDER: **You're acting funny,** *(name of Puppet 2).* **What are you trying to be, a robot?**

PUPPET 2: *(Talking like a robot.)* **Yes, I am a robot. What do you want me to do?**

PONDER: **I want you to find some berries for me to eat so that I don't have to look for them.**

PUPPET 2: *(Robot voice.)* **Find berries?**

PONDER: **Yes, find berries, especially strawberries, and bring them to me. They're yummy.**

PUPPET 2: *(Robot voice.)* **That does not compute.**

PONDER: **It doesn't compute, or you don't want it to?**

PUPPET 2: *(Robot voice.)* **That does not compute.**

PONDER: *(Laughs.)* **Okay, you win. It's too bad you're a robot. Your mother brought over your favorite food, but since robots don't eat, I'll have to give it away to another** *(type of animal Puppet 2 is).*

PUPPET 2: *(Robot voice.)* **Take me to the food.**

PONDER: **No. Robots don't eat food.**

PUPPET 2: *(Robot voice.)* **This robot eats food. I choose to eat food.**

PONDER: **Robots can't make choices. Only people can.**

PUPPET 2: *(Robot voice.)* **I am a different kind of robot.**

PONDER: **I'm afraid not. People can make good choices and bad choices. Robots can't make ANY choices.**

PUPPET 2: *(Robot voice.)* **I am a robot who makes good choices.**

PONDER: **I wish that were true, because making good choices pleases God. Making good choices is one way to show God you love him.**

PUPPET 2: *(Looks at Ponder, talking in normal voice.)* **Are you sure that robots can't make choices?**

PONDER: **Positive.**

PUPPET 2: **Then I guess I'm not a robot.**

PONDER: **That's a good thing. Did you quit being a robot so you could make choices that would please God?**

PUPPET 2: **Of course . . . AND I want to eat what my mom sent. Where is it?**

PONDER: *(Laughs.)* **Follow me. I'll show you.**

BP48: Trust Me

Cast: Ponder the Frog, Noah's Park Puppet 2

Props: Optional: a short board to place in the center of the stage as a "bridge"

Ponder and Puppet 2 are both at one side of the stage.

PUPPET 2: *This bridge is old.*

PONDER: *But it's safe. Animals cross it all the time.*

PUPPET 2: *I'm afraid. It might break if I try to walk across it.*

PONDER: *If you don't want to use the bridge, you can swim through the water with me.*

PUPPET 2: *I don't want to get wet.*

PONDER: *Then you'll have to stay on this side of the river.*

PUPPET 2: *But I want to go to the other side. It's filled with fruit trees, berry bushes, and acres and acres of tall grass.*

PONDER: *Then you have to cross the bridge.*

PUPPET 2: *But what if it breaks? What am I going to do?*

PONDER: *You're going to have to make a choice. Either you trust me and believe me when I say that it will* hold you, or you stay on this side of the bridge.

PUPPET 2: *I want to trust you. You're sure it will hold me, even if it looks rickety?*

PONDER: *Yes, even if it looks rickety.*

PUPPET 2: *Okay. Because you say it's safe, Ponder—and you're a very wise, old frog—I'll go across, even though I'm scared.* (Puppet 2 sidles inches, moving across the stage, testing each step. Finally it reaches the other side.) *Yeah! I made it. I'm here. I crossed the bridge!*

PONDER: (Ponder hops across the stage until it is next to Puppet 2.) *What you did took a lot of trust. The way you trusted me is the same way that people have to trust God to care for them. Sometimes it doesn't look like they're going to make it through problems, but then they do. When people trust God, it shows God that they love Him.*

PUPPET 2: *I'm glad I trusted you. Let's get going. I can't wait to start eating!*

PONDER: *Okay! I'm right behind you.*

(Exit together.)

BP49: Unhappy Jokes

Cast: Ponder the Frog, Noah's Park Puppet 2

Ponder and Puppet 2 are onstage.

PUPPET 2: *You should have seen Screech's face! He'll never forget that practical joke.*

PONDER: *No, I'm sure he won't. It's not every day that you wake up to find your tail tied into a knot.*

PUPPET 2: *(Laughs.) I wish I could have seen his face . . . What was that noise? (Looks all around, scared.)*

PONDER: *What noise? I didn't hear anything.*

PUPPET 2: *It's probably nothing. I have to be on the alert, though. Screech will try to get back at me.*

PONDER: *No doubt. Why do you play these practical jokes on each other?*

PUPPET 2: *Because we're friends.*

PONDER: *You have a strange idea of friendship.*

PUPPET 2: *What's your idea?*

PONDER: *I like what God says about loving each other. He wants me to love Him first and then love everyone else in the same way I love myself.*

PUPPET 2: *I love Screech.*

PONDER: *How can you say that you love him when you're always playing mean jokes on him?*

PUPPET 2: *I'm just having fun with him.*

PONDER: *Do you think it's fun to be scared of every sound until Screech gets back at you?*

PUPPET 2: (Thinks.) *No, that's not very fun.*

PONDER: *Wouldn't you like to have a friend who treats you the way you want to be treated?*

PUPPET 2: *That would be nice.*

PONDER: *Maybe you should talk with Screech.*

PUPPET 2: *I doubt if he'll listen to me. But I'd like to have a better friendship with him. I'll go find him now.*

PONDER: *Great. I think you'll be surprised at what comes from this.*

PUPPET 2: (Begins to walk away; then calls.) *Hey, Screech! I wanted to talk to—* (Suddenly, a handful of confetti is thrown at Puppet 2 from offstage. Laughing is heard offstage. Puppet 2 looks at himself covered in confetti, looks at the kids, looks at Ponder.)

PONDER: *Well, I DID say you'd be surprised, didn't I?* (Puppet 2 sighs and exits.)

BP50: How Many Times?

Cast: Ponder the Frog, Noah's Park Puppet 2

Note: Use a Noah's Park puppet other than Dreamer for Puppet 2.

Ponder and Puppet 2 are onstage.

PUPPET 2: *Thanks for getting up early to watch the sunrise with me.*

PONDER: *It's my pleasure. I like the peacefulness of the early morning.*

PUPPET 2: (*Both puppets start bobbing up and down as if the ground is shaking.*) *What's happening?*

PONDER: *I have no idea.* (*Both puppets turn their heads to the right and then all the way to the left as if watching something moving across the stage.*) *What is Dreamer the Rhinoceros doing up so early?*

PUPPET 2: *I don't know, but when he runs he shakes the ground where we're sitting. That's so rude of him.*

PONDER: *He probably doesn't know we're here.* (*Both puppets start shaking again.*)

PUPPET 2: (*Yells.*) *Dreamer, slow down. We're trying to watch the sunrise!*

PONDER: (*Both puppets pretend to watch Dreamer run from left to right.*) *I don't think he heard you. His hooves are drowning out your voice.*

PUPPET 2: *This is just great! That rhinoceros is ruining everything.*

PONDER: *Dreamer doesn't mean to ruin your morning. Forgive him, and let's make the best of it.*

PUPPET 2: *But he's run across the meadow twice. How many times am I supposed to forgive him?*

PONDER: *(Both puppets shake again.)* **Well, this is his third run.**

PUPPET 2: *(Puppets watch from right to left.)* **Why should I forgive him so many times?**

PONDER: *Learning to love one another isn't always fun, but it means that you keep on forgiving.*

PUPPET 2: *What if Dreamer runs across the meadow again?*

PONDER: *Then you forgive Dreamer again. Of course, we can move to another spot so that Dreamer won't get in our way, but it won't do much good.*

PUPPET 2: *Do you think he'll follow us?*

PONDER: *No, but while we were talking, the sun came up.*

PUPPET 2: *Oh, no!*

PONDER: *Let's watch the sunrise tomorrow morning on top of Nosy Rock instead of here.*

PUPPET 2: *Good idea! (Exit together.)*

BP51: My Turn, Your Turn

Cast: Ponder the Frog, Noah's Park Puppet 2

Props: A daisy (real or artificial)

Puppet 2 and Ponder stand by each other.

PUPPET 2: *(Counts one petal for each sentence.)* **It's my turn. It's your turn. It's my turn. It's your turn. It's my turn. It's your turn. It's—** *(Pause.)* **I forgot where I was. I'll start over. It's my turn. It's your turn. It's my turn. It's your turn. It's my turn. It's your turn.**

PONDER: *(Enters during the counting.)* **It is? What is it my turn to do?**

PUPPET 2: **Shh! I lost my place again.**

PONDER: **Did you need me to do something?**

PUPPET 2: **No. I've got to concentrate.**

PONDER: **About what?**

PUPPET 2: **About being first in line.**

PONDER: **What are you talking about?**

PUPPET 2: **I like being first in line, but my mother told me that I have to share. So, I want to be fair. Maybe today is my turn to be first in line, and maybe today is someone else's turn. I decided to count the petals of this flower to find out if it's my turn.**

PONDER: *Do you think the petals of a flower can really tell you when you should give up your place in line?*

PUPPET 2: *How else will I know that it's not my turn?*

PONDER: *One of the ways we learn to love each other is by cheerfully giving to those who have a need. Maybe you could look around you and see if someone else really wants to be the line leader. Or maybe there's someone who just needs to feel special today by being first.*

PUPPET 2: *Oh. I didn't think about that. That would be a lot easier.*

PONDER: *A lot easier than counting flower petals?*

PUPPET 2: *Yes. I didn't know what I was going to do in the fall when there were no more flowers. Thanks, Ponder.*

PONDER: *You're welcome,* (Name of Puppet 2).

PUPPET 2: (Turns to leave.) *Did you want to go in front of me?*

PONDER: *No, you go ahead, but thanks for asking.*

(Exit.)

BP52: Sharing Great Ideas

Cast: Ponder the Frog, Noah's Park Puppet 2

Ponder and Puppet 2 are onstage.

PUPPET 2: *Ponder, I'm so glad to see you. I need help.*

PONDER: *What's wrong?*

PUPPET 2: *Today we were learning about loving others. My teacher said that sharing what we have shows love.*

PONDER: *That's right.*

PUPPET 2: *I want to share what I have.*

PONDER: *Good.*

PUPPET 2: *But the problem is that I don't have anything.*

PONDER: *What do you mean you don't have anything?*

PUPPET 2: *My sister, brother, and I share all of our toys; so they're not mine to give away. And I don't own anything else. What can I share with others? I don't have anything. Now no one will think I love them.*

PONDER: *(Name of Puppet 2),* **you have a lot of things you can share.**

PUPPET 2: *(Looks around.)* **Where? I don't see anything.**

PONDER: *You have a smile.*

PUPPET 2: *Do you think that there are people or animals who want me to smile at them?*

PONDER: *I think there are a lot of people and animals who would like you to smile at them.*

PUPPET 2: *What else do I have?*

PONDER: *You have your friendship.*

PUPPET 2: *I can share that with people.*

PONDER: *And you tell great jokes; you listen to people who want to talk; and you're willing to help others.*

PUPPET 2: *I can share all of those things?*

PONDER: *Yes, you can, and you do.*

PUPPET 2: *Oh, good. Sharing myself with others is important. And you shared too just now!*

PONDER: *I did?*

PUPPET 2: *Yes, you shared your great ideas with me.*

PONDER: *Well, so I did! Let's go find some more people to share ourselves with.*

PUPPET 2: *Another great idea!*

(Exit together.)

NOTES

NOTES